SEARCH
TO
SOLD

*How Search Engine Optimization (SEO) Can
Double Your Service-based Business Revenue*

SERGE AUGUSTIN

Search to Sold

How Search Engine Optimization (SEO) Can Double Your Service-based Business Revenue

Disclaimer

No one can guarantee a #1 ranking on Google.

Beware of SEOs "experts" that claim to guarantee rankings, allege a "special relationship" with Google, or advertise a "priority submit" to Google. There is no priority submit for Google. In fact, the only way to submit a site to Google directly is through the URL Inspection Tool, by submitting a Sitemap, or for more specialized content, using the Google Indexing API. You can do any of these yourself.

Table of content

Table of content...3

Chapter One - The Digital Marketing Transformation.................. 6

My Story.. 7

The SEO and Local Marketing Masterclass............................. 9

Navigating Through the Chapters... 11

Chapter Two - Understanding SEO and Its Impact on Your
Business...14

The Essence of SEO...14

The Mechanics of Search Engines... 16

The SEO Advantages Over Paid Advertising............................ 18

The Fundamentals of SEO.. 20

The Evolution of SEO..22

Recap: SEO as a Growth Lever... 25

Chapter Three - Crafting Your SEO Strategy............................ 27

Laying the Groundwork..27

Market and Competitor Analysis.. 29

Keyword Research and Selection... 31

On-Page Optimization... 33

Off-Page Optimization...35

Recap: Building a Robust SEO Strategy.................................. 37

Chapter Four - Optimizing Your Website for Local Search..........41

The Local SEO Landscape..41

Site Architecture for Local Visibility..43

Content Localization..45

Technical Local SEO... 48

The Power of Local Reviews..50

Recap: Maximizing Local SEO Performance............................52

Chapter Five - Google MyBusiness Optimization for Local
Domination...55

Google Business Profile Essentials..55

Optimizing Your GBP Listing.. 57

Engaging with Customers on GBP.. 59

Leveraging GBP Insights...61

Advanced GBP Features and Opportunities................................. 64

Recap: Google Business Profile Mastery..................................... 66

Chapter Six - Enhancing Visibility with Citations and Directories..
69

The Impact of Citations on Local SEO...69

Selecting the Right Directories and Platforms.............................70

Crafting Consistent Citation Profiles...72

Monitoring and Updating Citations.. 73

Overcoming Common Citation Challenges...................................75

Recap: Citations as a Local SEO Tool...77

Chapter Seven - Building a Strong Online Reputation.................80

The Value of Online Reviews.. 80

Managing and Responding to Reviews...81

Encouraging Customer Reviews...84

Leveraging Testimonials and Case Studies...................................86

Reputation Management Tools and Practices................................88

Recap: The Pillars of Online Reputation..................................... 90

Chapter Eight - Content Marketing for Local Engagement..........93

Content as a Local Engagement Driver.. 93

Planning Your Content Strategy.. 95

Creating Locally Relevant Content...97

Distributing Your Content Effectively... 99

Measuring Content Success... 102

Recap: Content Marketing Mastery.. 104

Chapter Nine - Advanced Local SEO Techniques.......................107

Exploring Hyperlocal SEO.. 107

Schema Markup for Local Businesses..109

Mobile Optimization for Local Search....................................... 111

Local SEO for Voice Search.. 113

Leveraging Local Partnerships and Events.................................115

Recap: Navigating Advanced Local SEO....................................118

Chapter Ten - The Role of Call Tracking in Local Marketing.... 121

Overview of Call Tracking.. 121

Importance for ROI...122

Setting Up Call Tracking Systems... 123

Analyzing Call Data for Marketing Insights............................125

Optimizing for Phone Call Conversions...................................127

Integrating Call Tracking with Other Marketing Tools........... 129

Recap: Optimizing Client Acquisition Through Calls.............131

Chapter Eleven - Tracking Success and Measuring ROI.............134

Defining Success in Local Marketing.......................................134

Essential Tools for Tracking Local SEO Performance............ 135

Interpreting Data for Strategic Decisions................................. 139

Continuous Improvement and SEO Maintenance....................141

Demonstrating Value and ROI to Stakeholders....................... 143

Recap: Mastering Measurement and ROI.................................145

Conclusion- Consolidation of Core Concepts................................148

The Call to Continuous Growth... 150

Comprehensive Action Plan... 151

The Next Steps Forward... 154

Additional Resources for Success..155

The Digital Marketing Transformation

Digital marketing has changed a lot. It's not like the old days. Now, almost everyone uses the internet to find what they need. This is very important for businesses that offer services. Think of places like hair salons, plumbing companies, or law firms. People look online to find these services. So, these businesses need to show up when people search for them. This is where SEO comes in. SEO stands for Search Engine Optimization. It helps your business show up on the internet when people search for the services you offer. SEO is like a sign that tells people, "Hey, we are here!" It helps people find your business when they are looking for what you offer. For example, if you fix cars and someone's car breaks down, they go online and search for help. If you use SEO, they will see your car repair shop first. This is very good for your business. People will call you to fix their cars. This is why being seen online is so important. Now, you might wonder, "Why do I need to show up in local searches?" Well, for service-based businesses, your customers are usually close to you. They are in the same town or city. They are not far away. When they need help, they want someone nearby. So, if your business shows up when they search, they are more likely to choose you. This is what we call local visibility. It means people in your area can see your business easily online. Being visible locally can make a big difference. It can help your business grow. More people will know about you. More people will call you. And more people will buy your services. This is why digital marketing and SEO are so important. They help people find you. And when people find you, your business does better. You have made a great choice to read this book. This book will help you understand digital marketing and SEO. You will learn how to make your business show up online. This will help you get more customers. You will see how to make your business grow. This book has many good ideas. You can use these ideas to help your business. You will see how to make more people notice your service. This is a big step for you and your business. Reading this book shows you want to grow your business. It shows you are ready to learn new things. And it shows you are ready to work hard. This is very good. The things you learn from this book can change your business. They can help it grow. They can make you more successful. And they can make you feel proud of what you have done. Remember, doing well in business is not just about luck. It is about learning and working hard. It is also about being smart with digital marketing and SEO. This book will help you with all of that. You will learn how to use the internet to help your business. And you will learn how to do it in a way that is easy to understand. So, get ready to learn a lot. Get ready to work on your business in new ways. And get ready to see your business grow. This is an exciting time for you. Let's begin this journey to help your business shine online!

My Story

Hi, I'm Serge. You might be wondering how an ex-professional athlete like me ended up in the digital marketing world. I'm here to tell you all about it. My story isn't just a tale of personal change. It's about how I discovered the power of SEO and digital marketing and decided to use it to help other businesses grow. It's about the birth of Digileadgenbot and the difference it's making in the world of local business.

Back when I was an athlete, my focus was on performance, competition, and strategy. I learned that to win, you need more than just talent.

You need a plan. You need to know your strengths and how to use them. When I retired from sports, I didn't lose that drive. In fact, I carried it with me into the business world.

Let's talk about the beginning. It was 2016, and I realized that businesses, especially local service-based ones, were struggling to get noticed. I saw a need for a better way to get leads, and I knew I could help. That's when Digileadgenbot started to take shape. It was more than just a business idea. It was a passion to see small businesses succeed and to see them get the recognition they deserved.

Why SEO? Well, I saw that with SEO, businesses could grow without always paying for ads. They could be at the top of search results when people looked for their services. And the best part? It was like having a magnet that pulled in customers, even when you were sleeping. This was powerful, and it was something I wanted to become great at.

At Digileadgenbot, we don't just stop at SEO. No, we offer a full range of services to help businesses shine. Picture a box full of tools — except these tools are for growing your business online. We've got website design, content marketing, social media strategies, AI chatbots, audits, and reputation management. It's like your business gets its own superhero cape.

Here's something I've learned along the way: A well-ranked website is a gift that keeps giving. I've seen a website we worked on years ago continue to bring in customers every day. This is the kind of long-term success I want for every business we work with.

Service-based businesses are where we shine. There's something special about helping a business that helps others. When someone searches online and finds your service at the top of the list, that's a win for everyone. Your phone starts to ring, and you're there to provide the service they need. That's what we aim for with every client at Digileadgenbot.

And we're not keeping these secrets to ourselves. We're sharing them on our YouTube channel. It's packed with tips and tricks for businesses like yours. Think of it as your go-to spot for free advice on making your online presence count. Go ahead and hit that subscribe button. Let your business reap the benefits of our knowledge.

So, that's my story. It's about transition, growth, and a deep desire to see businesses thrive. As much as I love the world of sports, helping businesses grow with Digileadgenbot is now my main stage. And guess what? We're just getting started. There's an entire digital world out there waiting for your business to make its mark.

Are you ready to watch your business grow? Are you prepared to see your phone light up with customer calls? Reach out to me at serge@digileadgenbot.com. Let's talk about making your business the go-to name in your local market. It's time for your success story to begin.

The SEO and Local Marketing Masterclass

When you open a book, it's like opening a door to a new world. This book is your key to unlocking the power of SEO and local marketing for your service-based business. As you turn each page, you'll learn strategies that can help you find more customers. This is not just any marketing guide. It's a path to growth, to reaching more people who need your services, and to making your business shine in your local area.

Let's talk about why this matters. Think of your business. It's special, and you know it has so much to offer. Now, imagine more people in your town or city finding your business first when they search online for services you provide. That's what SEO and local marketing can do. They help people find you. They are like signs on a digital highway that guide customers to your door.

But why is this book different? It's because it's practical. Every chapter is filled with steps you can follow. It doesn't just tell you what to do. It shows you how. You want to grow your business, right? Then you need more than ideas. You need actions you can take today, tomorrow, and the next day. That's what you'll get here.

Why should you trust this book? Think about all the books and articles out there. They talk about marketing like it's a secret code. This book is not like that. It's written for you, using simple words and clear steps. It's like having a friend who knows a lot about SEO and local marketing explaining it all to you, over a cup of coffee, in words that make sense.

This book is also special because it sticks with you. As you keep reading, you'll find that you're learning new things. You'll see your business in a new light. You'll understand what makes your business stand out and how to tell the world about it. This is not just about getting customers for today. It's about building a business that lasts, that grows, and that continues to bring in new customers.

Each chapter of this book takes you deeper into the world of SEO and local marketing. You'll start with the basics, the building blocks. Then, step by step, you'll learn more advanced techniques. By the end, you'll not only know what to do but also why it works. And that's powerful. Knowing why means you can make smart choices for your business, every single day.

Reading this book is a promise to yourself. It's a promise to take your business seriously and to do what it takes to make it thrive. It's a promise to not just work in your business but to work on your business. And when you keep that promise, amazing things will happen. Your phone will ring more, your inbox will fill with inquiries, and your schedule will be busier than ever.

This book is like a toolbox. Each chapter gives you new tools. You'll learn how to use these tools to build a strong presence in your local market. You'll learn how to make sure that when people search for the services you offer, they find you. Not once or twice, but consistently. That's what makes a business strong. That's what keeps you in the game.

And remember, as you read this book, you're not alone. There are many other business owners out there, just like you, looking to grow. This book is for all of you. It's a guide you can come back to, time and time again. Whenever you're wondering what to do next to attract more customers, open this book. The answers will be waiting for you, ready to help you take the next step.

So, are you ready to begin? Are you ready to learn and to apply what you learn? Are you ready to see your business grow? If you said yes, then this book is for you. Let's dive in. Let's build something great. Together, we'll turn your service-based business into a local powerhouse. And it all starts with this SEO and Local Marketing Masterclass.

Navigating Through the Chapters

It's great to have you here. We're about to embark on a journey through this book, and I want to make sure you know exactly where we're headed. Think of this section as a map. A map that shows you all the stops we'll make on our trip through digital marketing and SEO. Don't worry, I'll be with you at every step, explaining everything in a way that's easy to get. Let's dive into the main lessons you're going to learn from each chapter.

Chapter one is our starting point. Here, you'll discover the ABCs of SEO. What is SEO? Why does it matter? How do search engines work? We'll talk about keywords, those important words people use to find stuff on the internet. I'll show you how to pick the right ones for your business. It's super important because it helps people who are looking for what you offer to find you. And when they find you, well, that's good for business.

Then, we move onto chapter two. This is where things start to get really interesting. You'll learn about your website and how to make it a place people want to visit. We'll cover topics like making your site look good on phones because lots of people use their phones to go online. We'll also talk about making your site easy for visitors to use. When they can find what they need without trouble, they're more likely to stick around.

In chapter three, we'll put on our detective hats. We're going to learn all about your competition. Why? Because knowing what others in your business are doing can help you do even better. You'll learn how to look at their websites and see what's working for them. Then you can use those ideas to help your own business grow.

Chapter four is all about content. Content is just a fancy word for the words, pictures, and videos on your site. Good content is like a magnet; it pulls people in. I'll show you how to make content that people want to read, watch, or look at. We'll also talk about how often to add new stuff to your site so people have a reason to come back.

By the time we reach chapter five, you'll be halfway through our journey. And that's where we focus on getting your name out there. We'll chat about things like social media - you know, like Facebook and Instagram. I'll tell you how to use these tools to talk to more people about your business.

Chapter six is about trust. Trust is huge. If people trust your business, they're more likely to become your customers. We'll go over how to build that trust through reviews and testimonials. These are the good things that people say about you, and they can be very persuasive to others.

Next up, chapter seven, we'll explore local SEO. This is all about making sure that people in your area can find you. If you have a shop or a local service, you want people nearby to come to you first. We'll cover how to show up in local searches, so you're the first option they see.

Chapter eight is when we'll talk about keeping track of how you're doing. It's called analytics. This is like a report card for your website. It tells you how many people come to your site, how long they stay, and what they look at. This info is gold because it helps you understand what's working and what's not.

In chapter nine, you'll learn about ads. Ads can be a fast way to tell more people about your business. But, we'll talk about how to do it without spending too much money. You'll learn to make ads that speak to the right people and grab their attention.

Finally, we'll wrap up our journey in chapter ten with a big picture look. We'll talk about putting all the pieces together. You'll learn how to make a plan that uses everything we've talked about. And I'll show you how to change that plan if you need to, keeping your business growing and attracting more customers.

That's our roadmap. Ten chapters full of lessons that are easy to understand and super useful. We'll take everything step by step, so you're never overwhelmed. You'll walk away from each chapter with clear, specific steps you can take to help your business shine. Ready? Let's make your business the star of the show.

Understanding SEO and Its Impact on Your Business

The Essence of SEO

Let's talk about SEO. It's something you might have heard of. It stands for Search Engine Optimization. This is a big deal if you have a business. It can help you get more people to see your website. It's like when you play hide and seek. SEO is like the friend that tells you the best hiding spots so you won't get caught. It helps your website stand out so people can find it easily on the internet.

Now, some folks think SEO is just a fancy trick. But it's not. It's very important. Think about it. When you want to find something, where do you look? Most of us go to a search engine like Google. If you want to find a plumber or a bakery, you type it in and see what comes up. The better your SEO, the higher your business shows up in those search results. That means more people can find you. And that's a good thing, right?

But SEO isn't just about being at the top. It's about being seen by the right people. People who are looking for what you offer. If your website is easy to find and gives people what they want, they will visit it more. They might even tell their friends about it. And when people like your site, they come back. That's good for business.

Think about a lemonade stand. If you set it up where no one goes, you won't sell much lemonade. But if you put it on a busy street where thirsty people walk by, they'll see your sign, stop, and buy a drink. SEO is like putting your stand on the busiest street on the hottest day. It helps the right people find you at the right time.

You might have thought that SEO is too complicated. That's another misunderstanding. It can take some time to learn, but once you know how it works, it's not that hard. You can even do some of it yourself. The key is to make sure your website has the right words and information that people are searching for. It's like using the right bait for fishing. Use the bait that the fish like, and you'll catch more fish.

SEO is also not just a one-time thing. It's something you keep doing. The internet changes a lot. New websites pop up. Old ones get updated. Search engines like Google change how they decide which sites to show first. So, you have to keep working on your SEO to stay in the game. It's like gardening. You can't just plant seeds and walk away. You need to water them, pull out the weeds, and sometimes move the plants to where they get more sun. That keeps your garden growing, just like SEO helps your business grow.

Here's something cool about SEO. It can work better and cost less than ads. Ads are like those flyers people hand out on the street. Most people just throw them away. But with SEO, it's like someone asking for a flyer because they want to know about your lemonade stand. They're already interested in what you have. So, you're not just throwing your money away. You're investing it in something that brings people who want what you're selling. That's smart, isn't it?

So, that's the essence of SEO. It's a powerful tool. It can help your business succeed. It's not magic, but it's pretty close. And the best part? It helps people who are looking for what you offer find you. It works day and night, and it can save you money in the long run. Now, that's a good deal for any business.

You might still have questions. That's okay. We can learn more together. SEO is big and ever-changing. But one step at a time, we'll get better at it. And as we do, your business can grow bigger and reach more people. That's what we all want, isn't it?

Remember, SEO is like the best hiding spot in a game of hide and seek. Use it well, and it can be a game-changer for your business. Keep it simple, keep learning, and soon, you'll see just how big a difference it can make.

The Mechanics of Search Engines

Search engines are like magic boxes. Now, when you want to find something on the internet, you type words into a search box. These words are called 'keywords'. The search engine takes these keywords and looks through many, many web pages. It finds the pages that have the same words you typed. That is how you get a list of pages, called 'search results'. But how does this really work? Let me tell you. It is a bit like a big library, but for the whole internet.

First, search engines have these things called 'crawlers' or 'spiders'. Think of them like little helpers. They go out and visit different web pages. When they find a page, they look at all the information. They read everything. They look at the words, the pictures, and even how the page is made. Then they take a note of what they find. They are like little note-takers for the internet.

After they take notes, they bring all the information back to the search engine. The search engine then puts the information in a big list. This list is called an 'index'. Think of it like a big book, where you can find information about all the web pages the crawlers visited. Now, when you type in keywords, the search engine looks in this big book. It tries to find the best pages that match what you are looking for.

But how does the search engine know which pages are the best? Well, the search engine has rules. These rules help to decide which pages are the most important. One rule is about 'keywords'. If a page has the same words that you typed, that page might be important. Another rule is about 'links'. If a lot of other pages link to a page, that means it might be a good page. So, the search engine uses these rules to make a list of the best pages for you.

Now, why is knowing this important for your business? When you know how search engines work, you can help them find your web page. You can use the right words that people are typing. You can make your page easy for the crawlers to read. When you do that, the search engine might think your page is important. It might show your page to more people. And more people visiting your page can mean more customers for your business.

So what can you do? You can make sure that your web page has the right keywords. You can also make sure that other pages link to your page. There are other rules too, but these are a good start. When you follow these rules, you can help the search engine find your page. This can help you grow your business without paying for ads. It is like getting a free sign for your shop that more people can see.

Remember, the internet is big. There are many pages, and everyone wants to be found. When you help search engines, you also help your business. You make it easier for customers to find you. And that is a very good thing for your business. So take a little time to learn about keywords and links. It can make a big difference.

Doing these things is called 'SEO'. It stands for 'Search Engine Optimization'. It means making your web page better for search engines to find. It is a very important skill for business owners. And it can help you grow your business in a big way. You don't have to learn everything at once. Start with keywords and links. Try to understand how the crawlers work. Make small changes to your page. And watch as more people come to visit.

Let's remember, all this takes time. You won't see changes right away. It's like planting a seed. You water it, you care for it, and then it grows. SEO is like that. You make changes, you wait, and then you see your business grow. So be patient and keep working at it. Your business can see amazing growth with the help of search engines. And that is something to be excited about.

The SEO Advantages Over Paid Advertising

When we look at the world of getting our name out there, two big words often come to the front: SEO and advertising. Let's talk about what makes SEO stand out. It's like having a shop that people walk into because they want to, not because they saw a flashy sign. Now, think about your own business. You want people to find you, to talk about you, and to keep coming back, right?

First, let's get one thing clear. SEO stands for Search Engine Optimization. It's a way to help your business show up when people search online. It's about making your website friendly to both people and search engines. We're talking about Google, Bing, or any place where you type in what you want to find.

Now, about ads. You know, the ones that pop up before a YouTube video or the banners on the sides of websites. Those are paid ads. You pay money, and your ad shows up in front of people. But there's more to understand.

Let's dig into why SEO might be a better choice for your business. One of the top reasons is money. Yes, money. With paid ads, you spend money every time someone clicks on your ad. The cost can add up fast. But with SEO, you put in the work up front, and the results can last a long time, without paying for each click. We like that idea, don't we?

And here's another thing. Trust. People tend to trust what comes up naturally in their search more than an ad. It's like when a friend tells you about a great place to eat vs. seeing a commercial for it. Which one would you trust more? That's the power of SEO. It's like your business being recommended by the search engine.

SEO isn't just about today or tomorrow. It's a long-term game. Think of it as planting a garden. You put the seeds in the soil, give them water and sunshine, and wait. With care and time, those seeds grow into plants. SEO is like that. You put in the effort, and over time, your website can grow into something that shows up when people search for what you offer.

But let's slow down for a moment. You might think, "Can't I just use both SEO and ads?" Sure, you can. They can work together. But if you have to choose where to put your effort or limited budget, SEO can give you more bang for your buck. It's like choosing between renting a fancy car for a day or buying a good car that's yours forever. The rented car is great, but once you stop paying, it's gone.

Now, think about your customers. They are smart. They know ads are ads. But when they search for something and find your website all by themselves, they feel good. It's their choice. They found you, and that feels more natural to them. It's a win for you because when they trust you, they stick around. They might even tell their friends about you. And that, my friend, is gold for your business.

Let's not forget how the world of the internet is changing. People search for things on their phones, tablets, and computers all day, every day. If your website is the one they find, and not just an ad that pops up and then disappears, you're more likely to be the one they call, visit, or buy from. It's about being there when they need you, not just when you pay to be in front of them.

So, what can you do with all this information? Start thinking about how you can make your website better for people and search engines. It's not just about throwing keywords around. It's about making sure your website is helpful, easy to use, and has the information people need. That's how you start with SEO. And that's how you start building a business that lasts, without paying for every click along the way.

Remember, SEO isn't a quick fix. It takes time and effort, but the results can last. It's like building a house. You start with a strong foundation, then you build it up, brick by brick. In the end, you have something solid that stands on its own. That's the kind of business you want, right?

So take a step back and look at your business. Think about the long-term. Think about trust. Think about being there for your customers when they're looking for you. That's the SEO advantage. It's more than just being seen. It's about being found, being trusted, and being the one they choose, again and again.

The Fundamentals of SEO

SEO stands for Search Engine Optimization. It's a powerful tool for your business. It helps people find your website when they search online. Imagine you have a store, but no sign. That's like a website with no SEO. People won't find you. SEO is like a big, bright sign that guides people to your store – your website.

First, keywords are important. They are the words people type into a search engine. If you fix cars, "car repair" might be a keyword for your business. When people search "car repair," you want them to find your website. So, you use those words on your site a lot. But not too much! That could look spammy, and we don't want that.

Now, let's talk about content. Content is all the stuff on your website. It's the words, the pictures, everything. Good content is useful and interesting. It answers questions people have. If your content is good, people will want to read it. Search engines will see that people like your site and show it to more people.

Links are another part of SEO. When other websites link to your site, it's like they are saying, "This site is good." Search engines see this and think your site must have good information. But these need to be good links from nice websites, not bad ones.

SEO also includes making sure your website works well. It should load fast. It should look good on phones, not just computers. If people visit your site and it's slow or looks bad, they might leave. That's bad for SEO.

We can't forget about local SEO. This is for businesses that have a physical spot where people come, like a store or an office. Local SEO is like telling search engines, "I am here!" You do this by putting your address and phone number on your website. And you make sure it's also on other websites, like online maps and business directories.

One of the best things about SEO is that it's fair. It doesn't matter how big or small your business is. If you do SEO well, you can be found just like the big companies. It's not like ads where the business with the most money wins. That's why SEO is great.

SEO takes time. It's not instant. You keep working at it. You keep making your website better. You keep adding good content and getting nice links. Over time, it works. Your website starts to show up when people search for things you are good at. And more people come to your website. This is good for your business.

Remember, SEO is not just about search engines. It's about people. People use search engines to find things. You want to help them find your website. You do that by using SEO to make your website a place where people can get what they need. When they find you, they might buy what you're selling.

Finally, it's important to keep learning about SEO. It changes. Search engines get smarter. They change how they decide which websites to show people. You need to keep up with this. If you keep learning and working on SEO, your website will keep doing well in the searches. And that means good things for your business.

Action steps to take for your business:

- Write down the main things you do or sell. These are your keywords. Use them wisely on your site.
- Create content that answers your customers' questions. Make it interesting and useful.
- Look for reputable websites that can link back to your site. Maybe you can write a guest post for a blog.
- Check your website speed. Make it fast. Make sure it looks good on a phone.
- Put your business address and phone number on your website clearly. Add it to online maps and directories.
- Keep track of your SEO progress. Use tools like Google Analytics to see how many people come to your site and from where.
- Set aside time each week to learn more about SEO and make improvements to your site based on what you learn.

Remember, SEO is a journey, not a race. Take your time. Do it right. And watch as it helps your business grow. It's powerful, and it's worth your time.

The Evolution of SEO

SEO, or Search Engine Optimization, is like a game. But not the kind of game you play once and then forget about. It's more like a sport where the rules can change at any time. You need to keep practicing and learning all the time. If you own a business and want people to find you online, you need to understand SEO. It's that simple. Think about a shop in a big city. If your shop is on a busy street, more people walk by and might come in to buy something. SEO is like the busy street on the internet. It helps people find your website when they search for something you offer. But SEO today is not the same as it was years ago. It has changed. A lot. And it keeps changing. When it started, people thought they could trick search engines into showing their websites first. They would stuff their web pages with the same words over and over. Or they would hide lists of words in the same color as the background. It was sneaky, and for a while, it worked. Then search engines got smarter. They started understanding what people were trying to do. They changed the rules. No more tricks. Now, search engines care about what is on your website and if it's good for people. They want to show websites that are helpful, easy to use, and have good information. So, if you have a business, you need to make sure your website is like that. It's like making your shop nice for customers, so they enjoy it and come back. If your website answers people's questions, if it's easy to read and understand, and if other people think it's good and link to it, search engines will like it. This means your website could show up higher when people search for what you offer. Search engines use many things to decide which websites to show. They look at words, but they also look at how new the information is and how people act on your website. Do they stay and read, or do they leave right away? They even look at if your website works well on phones because many people use their phones to search. Years ago, you could focus on just a few things and do well in search engines. Not anymore. Now you have to do many things well. You have to think about everything from the words and pictures on your website to how fast it loads. It's like being good at many sports at once. But why is this good for your business? Because when you make your website better for search engines, you are making it better for people, too. People trust search engines to find good websites. If your website is at the top, people might trust it more. They might think, "If Google shows this website first, it must be good." That can bring more people to your website. And some of those people will buy what you are selling. Making your website better for SEO is not just about search engines. It's about people. Remember, search engines don't buy anything. People do. If people like your website, search engines will too. Now, how do you make your website better? Start with good information. Write about what you know and what you offer. Make it easy and fun to read. Use words that people search for, but use them in a way that makes sense. Don't just list them. Write for people, not just for search engines. Your website also needs to be easy to use. People should find what they want quickly. If they don't, they will leave. And search engines notice that. Make sure your website works well on phones, too. Many people only use their phones to go online. If your website doesn't work on a phone, you lose those people. You also want other good websites to link to yours. This is like having friends in the city telling people about your shop. It shows search engines that your website is worth showing to more people. But be careful. The links need to be from good websites, not just any website. And you can't buy them. That's another old trick that doesn't work anymore. SEO is about understanding what people want and giving it to them on your website. It's about being honest and working hard to make your website good.

It's not about quick tricks. It takes time and effort, but it's worth it. If you do it right, more people will find your website, and your business can grow. Remember, SEO is always changing. You have to keep learning and improving. What works today might not work tomorrow. But the big idea is always the same: make your website good for people. That's the best way to make it good for search engines, too. If you do that, you can win the game of SEO.

Recap: SEO as a Growth Lever

Let's sit back and chat about what we've learned. We've talked about SEO and how it can really help your business grow. SEO helps people find your business online. It's like putting up big, shiny signs that guide customers to your door. But not just any door. The door to your website.

SEO is not just about getting more people to your site. It's about getting the right kind of people. The kind that are looking for what you offer. This means when they find you, they're more likely to stick around and maybe even buy something.

We saw that SEO is better than ads that you pay for. With SEO, you build something that lasts. Ads stop when you stop paying. But SEO keeps working for you, night and day.

Now, let's walk through the steps to use SEO for your business. These are simple things you can do right now:

- **Find the right keywords:** Think about what words people use when they look for your services. These are like magic keys that help them find you. There are tools online that can help you find these words.
- **Make your website friendly:** Make sure your website is easy to use

and nice to look at. If people like being there, they might stay longer. This matters to search engines.

- **Content is king:** Write about things that matter to your customers. Help them, teach them, and they will come to you. Keep your writing clear and simple.
- **Get the word out:** Tell people about your website. Use social media, emails, and other websites. If other sites think you're important, search engines will too.
- **Make friends with search engines:** Use tools like Google My Business to help search engines understand your website. This helps them show your site to the right people.
- **Keep learning:** SEO changes over time. Keep an eye on what's new. This way you can stay ahead and keep your website shining bright.

Remember, doing SEO is like planting seeds. You might not see the fruits right away. But with care and time, they will grow. And before you know it, you'll have a garden full of visitors ready to become customers.

Your website is like your online home. Make it welcoming. Make it a place people want to visit. Use words they search for. Make pages load fast. And make sure it looks good on phones, too. Because that's where a lot of your customers are.

As we close this chapter, think about one thing you can do today to make your website better. Just one. Could you write a new post? Could you check if your site works well on a phone? Pick something simple and do it. You'll be on your way to growing your business with SEO.

Remember, it's not magic. It's work. But it's work that can bring you rewards far into the future. It's about being there when people are looking for you. And not just being there, but shining bright, so they decide to stop by and see what you offer.

If you take these steps, and if you keep at it, SEO will work for you. It's like a good friend that keeps bringing people to your party. And the best part is, this friend doesn't get tired. It keeps working, even when you're asleep.

So, take a deep breath. Pick that one thing to do today. And step into the world of SEO. Your future customers are out there, searching for you. It's time to make sure they find you.

Crafting Your SEO Strategy

Laying the Groundwork

Before you dive into the world of SEO, it's like setting up a lemonade stand. You need to know why you're selling lemonade and who you want to sell it to. This is just like setting your SEO goals. You must figure out what you hope to achieve. It could be getting more people to visit your website. Or it could be to sell more of something, like shoes or services. Whatever it is, knowing your goal is the first step.

Now, let's talk about challenges. Imagine you're playing a video game. You have a mission. But there are obstacles in the way, like puzzles or bad guys. In SEO, challenges can be things like other websites that are also trying to get attention. Or maybe your website is new and nobody knows about it yet. You have to think about these things and make a plan. That's what overcoming SEO challenges is all about.

Identifying your SEO goals is like deciding on a destination before you start a trip. You need to know where you're going. Do you want to get more people in your city to know about your business? Or do you want everyone in the whole world to find your website? Once you know this, you can figure out which roads to take, or in this case, which SEO paths to follow.

Understanding SEO challenges is like knowing what to pack for your trip. You might need a raincoat if it's going to rain. Or maybe you need a map so you don't get lost. In the SEO world, you need to think about what could make your journey tough. Maybe you have a really common business name, and it's hard to stand out. That's a challenge. But don't worry, because once you know the challenges, you can get ready to face them.

Now, remember, you're not alone in this. Think of SEO like a team game. You have tools and people who can help you. You can use things like keywords, which are the words people type when they're looking for something online. You can also look at what other businesses are doing. This is like watching the best players to learn new moves. And you can always ask for help from friends or experts who know a lot about SEO.

It's important that your goals are clear. If you just want more people to click on your website, that's like saying you want more people to visit your lemonade stand. But what if they don't buy anything? That's why your goal should be not just more clicks, but the right clicks. People who really want what you're offering. This way, when someone visits your website, they are happy and might want to buy from you or learn more.

And when we talk about SEO challenges, it's not just about knowing they're there. It's also about not giving up. Even if it seems hard at first, you can do it. With a good plan and some hard work, you can make your website stand out, just like the best lemonade stand on the block.

Now, let's get practical. To identify your SEO goals, ask yourself some questions. Why do you have a website? What do you want it to do for you? Write down your answers. These are your goals. Keep them in front of you like a treasure map. They will guide you to where you want to go.

Next, think about your challenges. Write them down, too. Maybe your website is slow, and people don't like to wait. Or maybe there are so many other websites selling the same thing you do. These are your obstacles. But every obstacle has a way around it, or through it, and that's what your plan will help you find.

Remember, the internet is like a big city. There are lots of streets and lots of stands. But with the right goals and a plan for challenges, you can make your stand the one everyone wants to visit. So take these first steps seriously. They're the foundation of your SEO strategy, like the strong base you need to build a tall and sturdy tower.

Keep coming back to your goals and challenges. They might change as you learn more, and that's okay. It's like learning new tricks in a game. You get better, and you get closer to winning. So, start by laying this groundwork, and you'll be on your way to SEO success. Remember, it's all about the right preparation. And with that, you're ready to take on the world of SEO with confidence.

Market and Competitor Analysis

When you step into the world of SEO, it's like walking into a big, busy market. There's so much going on. People are everywhere. Some are selling fruits, some shoes, and some books. Now, you have your own little shop. How do you get people to come to you instead of the shop next door? That's where market and competitor analysis comes in.

Market analysis is a fancy term, but it's just looking around you. It's seeing what people like. What kind of shoes are they buying? Is it sneakers or sandals? Maybe they want rain boots because it's been rainy lately. You look at these things because it tells you what to put in your shop. It's like being a detective. But instead of solving crimes, you're solving puzzles about what people want.

This is important. Very important. Why? Because when you know what people want, you can give it to them. And when you give people what they want, they come to your shop. They might buy something. They might tell their friends about you. That means more people come, and your shop gets busy. That's good for you.

But it's not just about looking. It's about thinking too. When you look around the market, ask yourself questions. What's missing? What can you offer that nobody else does? Maybe everyone is selling black shoes, but no one has red ones. If you start selling red shoes, people who want to stand out might come to you. It's about being smart. This is called finding opportunities. It's like a treasure hunt. And the treasure is more people coming to your shop.

Now, let's talk about competitor analysis. This is when you look at the other shops. Maybe the shop that sells shoes just like yours. What are they doing? Do they have a big sign that people can see from far away? Do they have a sale going on? This is their strength. If people see their big sign, they might go there first. But it's not just about what they're good at. It's also about what they're not good at. Maybe their prices are high. Maybe their shoes aren't very nice. This is their weakness.

Why do you need to know their strengths and weaknesses? So you can be better. If their sign is big, make yours bigger or brighter or different. If their prices are high, maybe you make yours a bit lower. Not too low, because you need to make money too. But just low enough that people think they're getting a good deal at your shop.

Doing a competitor analysis is like playing a game. You have to think about what move to make so you can win. And winning means more people coming to your shop instead of the shop next door.

So, how do you do these things? How do you look around and think smart? You can start online. There are tools that tell you what people are searching for. It's like a list. If lots of people are searching for "red shoes," that's what they want. If nobody is selling them, that's your chance. You can also look at what shops are on the first page when you search for shoes. What are they doing? What can you do that's different or better?

But there's more to it than just looking. You have to keep your eyes open all the time. Things change. Maybe right now, everyone wants sandals.

But in a few months, it might be boots. You have to be ready to change what you offer. Always think about what's next.

And remember, this isn't a one-time thing. You can't just look around once and then stop. The market changes. People change. What they want changes. You have to keep doing your market and competitor analysis. Keep looking. Keep thinking. Keep asking questions. It's hard work, but it's worth it.

Here's what you can do right now. Go to your computer. Type in what you sell and see what comes up. Look at the first few websites. What are they doing? Write it down. Think about how you can do it differently. Then, look for what people are searching for. Write that down too. And then think about how you can give them what they want. That's your first step. It's a small step, but it's a start. And every big journey starts with a small step.

By doing this, you're learning. And when you learn, you get better. When you get better, your shop gets busier. And when your shop gets busier, you're winning. That's what you want. A busy shop. Happy customers. And a business that grows.

So, let's get busy. Let's look around. Let's be smart. And let's make your shop the one everyone wants to come to.

Keyword Research and Selection

When you create a website, you want people to find it. Think about a shop. If you open a shop, you want folks to come in, right? For your website, keywords are like a big sign that says, "Hey, come here!" They help people find your site when they use a search engine like Google.

Let's talk about finding keywords. Imagine you sell toys. You need to find words people use when they look for toys online. Some might type "fun toys for kids" or "affordable board games." These phrases are what we call keywords.

Finding the right keywords is not hard, but it's important. You start by thinking about what you sell. Let's stick with the toys example. You make a list of all the toy types you know. Then you look at this list and think about what words people might use to find these toys. Maybe "educational toys" or "action figures" are on your list. These could be good keywords.

Now, how do we choose from this list? We choose keywords that lots of people search for but not too many other websites use. It's like finding a sweet spot. If you pick a keyword that too many other sites use, your website might get lost in the crowd. But if you choose a keyword nobody searches for, then no one will find your website.

So, we need tools to help us. We can use tools like Google's Keyword Planner. It's free. It tells you how many people search for a keyword and how many other sites use it. We look for words with many searches but not too much competition. That's our sweet spot.

After we pick our keywords, we make sure we use them on our site. We put them in places like the title of the page, the headings, and in the text. But we don't stuff them in too much. If you put too many keywords on a page, it's not nice to read, and search engines don't like it.

Using the right keywords helps the right people find your website. It's like they're using a map, and your keywords are the big red X that says, "You are here." It's very important to pick the right keywords so that your website can be found by people who want to buy what you sell.

Here's something you can do right now. Open up a document and start making a list of all the things you sell or all the services you offer. Then, think about how someone might search for each one. Write down those ideas. Those are your potential keywords. Next, check these words in a free tool like

Google's Keyword Planner. Look for words with lots of searches but not too much competition. Choose the best ones for your website.

Remember, keywords are powerful. They can help people find your shop in the huge mall that is the internet. Use them wisely, and watch your website become a place where lots of visitors come to see what you have to offer.

On-Page Optimization

On-page optimization is about making sure that everything on your website is set up just right. It's like making sure that your shop front is inviting and that everything inside is easy for customers to find. This is important because search engines, like Google, want to show the best shops to people who are looking. Now, let me walk you through how you can make your website the best it can be.

First, let's talk about content optimization. This means creating content that both people and search engines love. Good content helps people and search engines understand what your website is about. It's like if you walk into a shop and everything is neat and labeled, you know exactly where to find what you need. The same goes for your website. You want your content to be clear, to the point, and helpful.

Here's what you should do. Write about things that you know people are interested in. Be helpful and answer questions that they might have. Write it in a way that's easy to read, like you are talking to a friend. Make sure you put the most important information at the top. And use headings to break up the text so it isn't just one big block of words.

Next up is site structure. This is about how your website is put together. It's like how a shop is laid out. You wouldn't hide the best-selling items in the back where no one can find them, right? In the same way, you want to make sure that the most important pages on your website are easy to find and get to. This makes it easy for people and search engines to see what you offer.

To do this right, make a plan of your website that looks like a tree. At the top of the tree is your homepage. Below that, you have the main sections or categories. Under those, you put all the pages that fit in each section. Make sure that every page is only a few clicks away from the homepage. This helps search engines find all your pages and understand how they are connected.

A good rule to follow is to link your pages to each other. This is like in a shop where an aisle for bread might have a sign pointing to the jams and spreads. On your website, if you talk about one thing on a page, link it to another page that talks about something related. This helps people stay on your website longer because they find more things that interest them.

Lastly, always check that everything on your website works. All the links should take people to the right pages. Pictures and videos should load fast and look good. And your website should be easy to use on phones, not just computers. More and more people use their phones to look at websites, so this is really important.

Remember, the goal of on-page optimization is to make your website the best it can be for both people and search engines. If you take care of your content and site structure, you help people find what they are looking for. And when people can find what they need, search engines will see your website as a good place to send people. This can help your website show up higher in search results, which means more people can find your business.

I've just shared with you some clear steps to take. It's important to put these into action. Start by looking at your website and thinking about the content and the structure. Make a plan to improve these, and then get to work on making those changes. It might take some time, but it's worth it. Remember, every little change you make can help your website be seen by more people.

Take your time with this. Go through your website page by page. Check the content. Make sure it's helpful and easy to read. Look at how the pages link to each other. Make sure it's easy for people to find their way around. And check that everything works, especially on phones. If you do all this, you'll be on your way to a website that works better for everyone.

And that's it! You now know the basics of on-page optimization. It's time to take these steps and use them on your website. When you do, you'll be making it easier for people and search engines to see just how great your business is. So, take a deep breath, roll up your sleeves, and start making your website the best it can be. Remember, the work you do here can make a big difference in helping people find you online. Good luck!

Off-Page Optimization

Now, let's step outside the boundaries of your website. Off-page optimization, it's like the word of mouth of the online world. It's how your site gets a nod from other places on the internet. This is crucial because it tells search engines, "Hey, this content over here is valuable, and people trust it." It's a green light for credibility and trustworthiness. So, let's dive into two major parts of off-page optimization: link building strategies and social signals.

First up, link building strategies. Think of the internet as a bustling city and links as roads leading to your shop. The more roads you have, the more likely people are to find you. In the digital landscape, links from other websites to yours are these roads. They not only bring visitors but also boost your reputation in the eyes of search engines. You see, when another website links to yours, it's like they're saying, "We trust this content enough to send our visitors to it." Search engines pick up on this trust and may rank your website higher as a result.

But how do you get these links? It's not just about any links; you want quality links from reputable sites. One way is through creating content that's so good, others can't help but share it. This could be a well-researched article, a helpful guide, or even an infographic. When you create something useful, others in your industry will want to point their readers your way. You can also reach out to websites and suggest where your content could add value to their pages. This is where it gets hands-on. Craft a personalized email, focus on how your content benefits them and their audience, and politely ask for a link.

Another method is guest posting. Write an article for another site in your niche. This gives you a chance to showcase your expertise and include a link back to your site. It's a win-win. You provide valuable content for them, and in return, you get a link and exposure to their audience. But remember, always aim for quality over quantity. One link from a top-notch site is worth much more than several from less reputable ones.

Now, let's shift gears to social signals. Social signals are like the buzz around your brand on social media platforms. They cover the likes, shares, and comments your content receives. These interactions hint to search engines that people are engaging with your content, which can help your rankings. Social media doesn't directly impact SEO, but the indirect effects are significant. Each share is a chance for someone new to see your content, visit your site, and maybe even link to it from their own site.

But it's not just about posting and hoping for the best. It's about engaging with your audience. Respond to comments. Thank followers for sharing your content. Join conversations. Create posts that inspire interaction, like asking questions or running polls. Connect with influencers in your niche who might share your content with their followers. It's these human touches that can amplify the reach of your content.

And here's something actionable for you. Start with a content calendar for your social media posts. Plan out what you'll share and when. Mix in your blog posts, helpful tips, industry news, and ask for feedback from your audience. Use tools to schedule your posts, so you're consistently present on social media. Consistency is key to staying on the radar of your followers and search engines.

Remember, off-page optimization is about building relationships and trust. It's about creating a web of connections through high-quality links and engaging social media presence. It's these connections that can turn the tide in your favor, making your website a go-to resource in your field.

So there you have it. A deep dive into off-page optimization. By focusing on building quality backlinks and creating a strong social media presence, you're telling the world and search engines that your website is a credible, authoritative source of information. Take these steps, put in the work, and watch as your online presence grows. It's a process, but the results are worth every effort you put into it.

Recap: Building a Robust SEO Strategy

So, we've been on quite a journey together, haven't we? We've learned a lot about SEO and how it can help your business reach more people. Now, let's make sure we've got all the steps down. This way, you'll be able to check off everything you've done and see if anything's missing. It's like looking at a map after a long trip to see all the places you've been.

First off, remember, SEO is a big deal for your business. It's like a sign that guides people to your shop instead of letting them just walk by. It's all about getting your website to show up on Google when people look for things you offer. So, let's make sure your sign is bright and clear for everyone to see.

Let's go over what makes a strong SEO strategy, step by step:

- Set clear goals: Know what you want from SEO. Do you want more people visiting your website, more calls, or more people walking into your store? Write down your goals.

- Understand what could go wrong: SEO isn't always easy, and things can get in the way. Maybe your website is new, or maybe lots of other businesses are trying to get noticed too. Think about these things so you can find ways to get ahead.

- Learn about your market: Look around at what people want and what other businesses are doing. This helps you see where you can fit in and stand out.

- See what others are doing: Look at other businesses like yours. What are they good at? What could they do better? Learn from them – without copying them, of course.

- Find the right words: These are the words people type into Google when they're looking for what you offer. Think about what words make the most sense for your business.

- Pick the best words: Not all words are equal. Some words might have too many other websites using them, and some might not have enough people looking for them. Choose words that are just right for you.

- Make your website nice for both people and Google: Your website should be easy to read and understand. It should also be set up so Google can find it easily.

- Arrange your website well: Make sure your website is neat. Like a tidy room, everything should be in its place so people and Google can find what they need.

- Get friends for your website: These are other websites that link to yours. It's like they're saying, "Hey, check this out, it's good!" This helps Google see that your website is worth showing to people.

- Be social: Use places like Facebook and Twitter to talk about your business. This also helps more people find you.

  Now, here's a handy list to make sure you're doing everything right:

- Write down your SEO goals on a piece of paper and put it where you can see it every day.

- Make a list of things that could make SEO hard for you and think of ways to beat those challenges.

- Do some homework on your market and competitors, maybe with some help from the internet or even a local library.

- Create a list of words you think people would use to find a business like yours. Ask friends or family if those are the words they would use too.

- Choose your words carefully, like picking apples from a tree – look for the ones that are just right.

- Check your website to see if it's easy to read and if everything is easy to find. Maybe ask someone who's never seen it before to take a look.

- Ask other business owners or friends with websites if they can link to your site. Just make sure their websites are nice and helpful too.

- Talk about your business on social media, and be friendly and helpful so people want to share what you post.

Doing all these things is like building a strong house. You start with a good foundation, and then you build it up, step by step. And remember, you don't have to rush. Take your time to do it well.

With this plan, you're ready to help your business grow with SEO. It's like a treasure map. Follow it, and it can lead you to more people finding your business. And when they do, they'll see how great your business is. That's what we all want, right?

So, there you have it. A full plan to help people find your business online. It's a big list, but you can do it, one step at a time. And if you follow these steps, you'll be on your way to having a website that's like a beacon – shining bright and guiding customers right to you.

Optimizing Your Website for Local Search

The Local SEO Landscape

When you have a business, you want people to find it. Especially if you run a shop or provide a service in a certain town or city. You want to be the one they call or visit when they need something you offer. This is where something special called local SEO comes into play. Let's dive in and see what this is all about.

Local SEO is like a helpful guide that tells people in your area about your business. Think of it as putting a big, bright sign that says, "Hey, we're here, and we've got what you need!" Imagine someone looking for a plumber. If you're a plumber, you want them to find you first. That's what local SEO can help with. It makes sure that when someone nearby searches for a plumber, your name pops up. It makes it easy for your neighbors to find you online.

Now, you might think, "But I already have a website. Isn't that enough?" It's a good start, but there's more to it. Just like your home needs the right address and directions to get to it, your website needs certain things to help people find it. This is where local SEO shines. It's about making it super clear to search engines, like Google, that your business is located in a specific place and ready to serve the local folks.

Here's why local SEO is so important. Most people use the internet to find what they need. They might type "best pizza in town" or "24-hour pharmacy near me." If your business is related to what they're searching for, you want to show up in those search results. Local SEO helps you do that. It's a way to tell search engines, "I'm here, and I have just what these people are looking for!"

Local SEO is different from general SEO. General SEO is like casting a wide net to catch many fish in the big ocean. Local SEO is more like fishing in a small pond where you know there are fish that like what you're offering. For local SEO, you need to focus on things that tell everyone you're part of the community. It's like joining the local parade or having a booth at the town fair. You get to show your local spirit and let people know you're one of them.

One big part of local SEO is being listed in directories. It's like being in the phone book back in the old days. When someone looks up something, you want your business to pop up with the right details. It should have your address, phone number, and other info that helps people reach you. This information should be the same everywhere it appears. It helps search engines trust you and show your business to more people.

Another part is about what people say about you. Reviews matter a lot. When people say good things about your service or products, it's like they're telling their friends to check you out. Search engines pay attention to this. They think, "Hmm, if people like this place, it must be good. Let's show it to more people!" So, it's important to have happy customers and encourage them to share their experiences online.

Keywords are also a big deal. These are words and phrases people use when they're looking for something. For local SEO, you want to use words that connect your business to your area. For example, if you sell flowers, you'd want to include "fresh flowers in [Your Town]" on your website. It helps search engines understand what you offer and where you are. This way, they can match you with people looking for fresh flowers in your town.

Your website needs to be friendly to both people and search engines. It should look good, work well, and have all the information folks need to know about what you do. It should also tell search engines about your business in a way they understand. This means using the right words, having your address clear and easy to find, and lots of other little things that add up to make a big difference.

So, to sum it all up, local SEO is a way to help people in your area find you online. It involves being listed correctly, getting good reviews, using the right keywords, and having a website that's helpful and clear. It's super important for your digital marketing strategy. It's how you make sure that when someone in your town is looking for what you offer, you're the answer they find. It's about connecting with your community and being the go-to choice for locals. And that's what can make your business grow and thrive.

Now that we've covered the basics of local SEO, let's make sure we put this into action. Check your website. Is your address easy to find? Are your services and products clearly listed? Do you mention your town or city on your pages? Are people reviewing your business? These are the first steps to take. Make these things happen, and you're on your way to being a local favorite. Remember, it's all about letting your neighbors know you're there and ready to serve them. And that's what local SEO helps you do, step by step.

Site Architecture for Local Visibility

Think of your website as your online home. Just like a physical store where each section has a purpose, your website needs clear rooms or sections too. This is how you help people find what they need fast. And when it comes to being spotted by locals, this becomes even more important.

Now, let's chat about design principles. Keeping things simple is key. A clean layout, with easy navigation, helps visitors. It also helps search engines understand your site. This means they can show your site to people searching for what you offer in your area. Think of it like putting up a big, clear sign in your store window.

You want to make sure your site structure is easy to follow. Start with a clear menu. Use big headings for different parts of your site, like 'Services', 'Contact', and 'About Us'. Under 'Services', list what you do. If you fix cars, you might have 'Oil Change', 'Brake Repair', 'Tire Services', and so on. This makes it easy for people to find the help they need.

But that's not all. Your website's content needs to be organized too. When you write about what you do, use words people in your town use. Mention local landmarks or events, but only if it makes sense. It helps people feel at home. And makes search engines see you're really part of the local community. You want to show up when neighbors search for services you offer.

Here's something you can do right now. Take a look at your website. Imagine you know nothing about your business. Can you find all your services easily? Are they sorted in a way that makes sense? Make sure every service you offer has its own spot on your site. This is not just good for visitors, but also for search engines.

Remember, every little change you make helps people find you. And it helps search engines understand that you're the local expert in what you do. Keep your site clean, clear, and with a focus on your local area. This way, you're not only helping your neighbors find great services. You're also growing your business. And that's something to be proud of.

So, here's what you can start with. Check your menu. Is it simple? Are your services easy to find? Is there a section about your community work or local news? If not, add it. Make sure your contact page has your local number and address. This tells everyone, including search engines, you're right there, in the neighborhood.

Remember, the goal is to make sure locals think of you first. When they need what you offer, you'll be the first name that comes to mind. By having a website that's clear and screams local, you're on your way to being the local go-to.

Take the time to get this right. Review your site often. Make changes if something isn't as clear or local as it could be. This isn't a one-time task. It's an ongoing effort to make sure your online home is inviting and relevant to your local community. Keep tweaking, keep improving, and you'll see the benefits in the attention you get from locals and the search engines alike.

And there you have it. A simple, clear path to making your website a local favorite. Try these steps. See how they help you connect with your community. Remember, every step you take makes a difference. So go ahead, make those changes, and watch your local visibility grow.

Content Localization

When we speak to our friends, we talk about the places we know. We mention the street corner where the coffee tastes just right. We talk about the park where the trees turn a golden hue in the fall. That's how we create a bond. Now, think about your website. Does it talk to your local audience like a friend would? Let's see how we can make that happen.

Your website is like your home online. It's where people come to visit you. They want to know what you're about, what you can do for them, and if you're a part of their community. They're looking for a local friend in the business they need. So, your website needs to talk the local talk.

First, think about the words you use. If you're a plumber in Atlanta, you don't just fix pipes. You fix pipes in Atlanta. It's not just about what you do. It's about where you do it. You want to be the plumber for Atlanta. So, your website should mention Atlanta a lot. But not just Atlanta. Mention neighborhoods, local landmarks, and events. This shows visitors you're one of them.

Now, let's dig deeper. You've got pages on your site. They tell people about your services. But do they link you to your town? Let's say you have a page about fixing leaky faucets. Don't just say you fix faucets. Say you fix leaky faucets in the Old Fourth Ward district. Share a story about a time you fixed a leaky faucet on Ponce de Leon Avenue right before the big parade. This makes your service real for the people who live there. They can picture it because they know these places.

What about blogs or articles? They're great for sharing helpful tips and stories. Write about how the local weather can affect homes. Talk about preparing for Atlanta's summer heat or how to deal with those sudden heavy rains. This isn't just helpful. It tells people you understand the local challenges. It makes them trust you.

But there's more. Ever hear someone talk and think, "They're not from around here?" The words we use can give us away. If you're in the South, maybe you say "y'all" instead of "you guys." It's subtle, but it matters. If your website uses the local language, it feels homey. It feels right to the people who live there. They feel like you're one of them because you sound like them. This is good. It makes them want to choose you.

Now, keywords. These are the words people type into Google when they're looking for someone like you. They're how people find you. If you're a bakery, they might search for "best birthday cakes." But if they're in Miami, they'll search for "best birthday cakes in Miami." See the difference? You need to know what people in your area type when they look for what you offer. Then, you use those words on your website.

How do you find these magic words? Think like your customer. Or even better, talk to them. Ask them what they'd type into Google. There's also tools online that can help you find these words. Use them. Once you have them, sprinkle them into your website text. Not too much. Just enough so Google knows where you are and what you do.

Here's something fun. Do you know those little events that happen in your town? Like the yearly strawberry festival or the big high school football game? Talk about them on your site. Write about how your business gets involved. Maybe you donate cupcakes to the bake sale or offer a discount when the local team wins. This doesn't just show you're a part of the community. It gives people a reason to cheer for you, too.

Let's talk about your contact page. It should have your address, yes. But it should also have a local flavor. Show a picture of your storefront with the local mural painted on the side. Mention that you're right across from the library, where the kids' story hour is a hit. When people see this, they don't just see an address. They see a neighbor.

So, we've talked about a lot. Local language, local events, and keywords. But here's the thing. You can't just throw them onto your site any old way. They need to fit like pieces in a puzzle. Each part of your website should have a touch of local flavor. But it should all come together to show one thing: you are the local choice for what they need.

Remember, when you write your website text, you're not just listing services. You're talking to your neighbors. Keep it warm. Keep it friendly. And keep it local. This way, when someone in your area needs what you offer, they don't just find a service. They find a local friend. Someone they'd like to do business with. And that, my friend, is how you win the local game.

Technical Local SEO

When we speak of local SEO, we must consider the technical side. This is about making it easy for search engines to understand where you are and what you do. Think of it as giving clear directions to a friend. You wouldn't just say, "Come to my place." You would give them your exact address and maybe even some landmarks. That's what technical SEO is like for your website.

For starters, let's talk about something called schema markup. This might sound fancy, but it's really not. Schema markup is a code that you put on your website. It's like a secret language that only search engines understand. It tells them all about your business. Like what kind of business you are, where you're located, and even when you're open.

Why is this important? Well, when search engines understand your business better, they can show your website to the right people. Imagine someone is looking for a bakery nearby. If your website says you're a bakery with the help of schema markup, you're more likely to show up in their search. It's a simple way to help the right customers find you.

So, how do you add schema markup to your website? First, you need to find the right code. You can use online tools that help you create it. They're like a form. You fill in your business details, and they give you the code. Then, you take that code and put it in the right spot on your website. If you're not sure how to do this, you might want to ask for help. But once it's done, it's a big step forward for your local SEO.

Another thing that's part of technical SEO is making sure your website is easy for search engines to look at. This means having a clean website structure. Think about a tidy room. Everything has its place, and it's easy to find what you need. That's how your website should be.

Your website should load fast, like a sprinter. People don't like to wait, and neither do search engines. If your website is slow, people might leave before they even see what you have to offer. There are tools online that can help you see how fast your website is. If it's slow, they can often tell you what's making it that way. Maybe your pictures are too big, or you have something fancy that doesn't need to be there.

Let's not forget about your website's mobile-friendliness. Nowadays, a lot of people use their phones to look things up. Your website needs to work well on phones, not just computers. It should be easy to read and easy to use, no matter how big someone's screen is. You can check this by looking at your website on your own phone. Is it hard to read? Do you have to zoom in a lot? If so, it's time to make some changes.

Finally, let's talk about local keywords. These are words that people use when they're looking for businesses like yours in their area. For example, "best coffee in downtown Toronto" is a local keyword. You want to make sure these kinds of words are on your website. But they need to be there in a natural way, like how you talk to a friend. Don't just put a list of cities you serve at the bottom of your page. Write about how you love serving coffee to the Toronto community, and mention some local events you've been part of. That way, you're telling search engines and people about your local connection.

Remember, technical local SEO is about helping search engines help you. By using schema markup, having a clean and fast website, being friendly to phone users, and using local keywords in a natural way, you're doing just that. It's like giving a friendly nod to search engines and saying, "Hey, I'm here, and I'm exactly what you're looking for." When you do this right, you're more likely to meet your neighbors online, the ones who are searching for a business just like yours.

Now, take a look at your website. Is it friendly to search engines and people in your community? If not, it's time to roll up your sleeves and make some changes. Start with schema markup, then move on to speed and mobile-friendliness. And don't forget about those local keywords. Take it one step at a time, and soon, you'll see the difference it makes.

The Power of Local Reviews

When we talk about local reviews, we are diving into something big. Reviews are words from people who have used a service or bought something. They tell others what they think about it. This is super important for any business, but even more for your local business. Let's find out why.

First, think about when you want to buy something or get a service for yourself. Maybe you want to eat at a new restaurant. What do you do? You might ask your friends or you might look online to see what people say about that place. That's exactly what reviews are. They are like your friends telling you, "Hey, this place is great!" or maybe, "No, this place is not good." Those words can help you decide to go or not to go.

Now, for your local business, reviews are like gold. They can make people come to you. Why? Because people trust what other people say. If lots of people say your business is awesome, then more people will want to come to see for themselves. It's simple but powerful.

So, how do you get these reviews? You ask for them. Yes, you just ask your customers to tell others about their experience. But there is a right way to do this. You can talk to your customers after you give them your service. Or you can send them a message saying, "Thank you for coming! Can you share your thoughts with others?" Make it easy for them. Give them a link where they can click and write their review.

Now, you have these reviews. What do you do with them? You show them to everyone. You can put them on your website. Make a special place for them where people can see what others say about you. This can help new people trust you even before they meet you.

Here is something else that's really cool. Reviews can help your business show up better in search results. Yes, when people look for something you offer, your business can come up higher on the list if you have good reviews. Search engines like Google think, "Hmm, people like this place. Let's show it to more people."

But wait, it's not just about having good reviews. Sometimes you might get a bad review. It can happen, and it's okay. What you do next is what matters. You need to respond to that review. Say you're sorry and try to make it better. This shows everyone that you care about your customers. And that's a big deal. People like businesses that care.

Let's go over some steps you can take to get and use reviews:

- Ask every customer for a review. Do it nicely and at the right time.
- Make a place on your website for reviews. Make it easy to find and read.
- When you get reviews, say "Thank you!" to the person who wrote it.
- If you get a not-so-good review, don't worry. Just respond in a kind way and try to fix it.
- Keep getting more reviews. The more you have, the better it is for your business.

There's one more thing you should know. People can leave reviews on other sites too, like Google or Yelp. Make sure you check these places because what people say there is also very important. If you see a review, respond to it. Even if it's a simple thank you. This shows you are paying attention.

So now, you understand how much power local reviews have. They can really change how people see your business. And they can bring more customers to you. That's something you can do right now. Start asking for reviews and see how your business grows. It's a small step, but it can lead to big things for you and your local business.

Remember to keep getting these reviews. It's not something you do just once. It's something that keeps on giving. It's like planting seeds that grow into big trees. Those trees are the good things that come from people saying nice things about your business. So keep planting those seeds, and watch your business grow.

And that's all about local reviews. They are important, and they can help you a lot. Use them well, and they will be a big help in making your business shine in your community.

Recap: Maximizing Local SEO Performance

So, we've covered a lot of ground together. We've talked about how to shine in local search results. This is big. It's a game changer for any service that wants to grab the attention of people nearby. Let's take a moment to look back at what we've learned.

Every step we've taken has been about making your website the go-to spot for your local area. It's like setting up a big, friendly sign that says, "Hey, look here! This is exactly what you're looking for, right around the corner!" That's what optimizing for local search is all about.

Remember the local SEO landscape we talked about? That's your foundation. It's understanding that the online world can bring real, live people through your door. People who are just around the block, looking for what you offer.

We dived into site architecture, too. That's how your website is built. It's like the blueprint of a house, but for your online home. We learned that a well-organized site helps people and search engines find what they need, fast. That makes everyone happy.

Then we got into the nitty-gritty of content localization. Here's where it gets personal. It's about talking to your community in their language, about their events. It's what makes your website feel like it's part of the neighborhood.

In technical local SEO, we got our hands dirty with the behind-the-scenes stuff. We added special codes to help search engines understand where you are and what you do. It's like giving Google a map to your front door.

And let's not forget the power of local reviews. They're gold. People trust what others say about you. So we found ways to collect those words of praise and show them off to the world.

Now, let's wrap it all up with some concrete steps you can take. This is where you turn what we've talked about into real results. Here's your checklist. Do these things to make your local SEO soar:

- Make sure your website tells people where you are. Put your address and local phone number on every page.
- Use local landmarks and language in your content. It shows you're part of the community.
- Get your business on local directories. It's like signing up for a town fair. You want a booth where people can find you.

- Add those special codes - Schema markup - to your site. They help search engines understand your local info.
- Encourage happy customers to leave reviews. Then, show these reviews on your site. It's social proof that you're great at what you do.
- Check that your site works well on phones. People use them all the time to find local services.

Doing all this will help people in your area find you when they search online. It's about being visible in your community's digital space. Take the time to get these steps right, and you'll see the difference.

That's it. You've got this. Now go out there and make your website a local favorite!

Google MyBusiness Optimization for Local Domination

Google Business Profile Essentials

Google Business Profile. You might have heard it buzz around in chats about local business growth. It's a big deal. Let's talk about what it is, why it matters, and how to use it for your local business.

Every local business wants to be seen. When people in your area search for the services you offer, you want them to find you, right? That's where Google Business Profile comes in. It helps your business pop up on Google when people nearby are looking for what you have. This is something called local SEO or local search engine optimization. It's about being visible to those in your neighborhood, city, or region.

Think about it like this. When someone searches on Google for a coffee shop, a plumber, or a pet store, they often use phrases like "near me" or "in [their city]." Google uses the information in your Google Business Profile to show your business as an option. Imagine you have a coffee shop. If your profile tells Google all about your shop, when someone searches for "coffee near me," your shop could appear as a suggestion. That's what we want.

So, what can you put in your Google Business Profile? A whole lot! You can show your business's name, location, and hours. You can add pictures of your storefront or the delicious food you serve. You can tell the story of your business in a description. You can even share posts about events or special offers. Every bit of information helps people know what you offer and how to find you.

A well-filled-out profile makes it easy for potential customers to choose your business over others. They can see your opening hours, where you are, and what other people think of you through reviews. It's a way to connect without even meeting in person. And in a world where so many choices are made online, this connection is key.

Reviews, oh, they're important. They're like gold. When someone says good things about your business, it tells others that you're trustworthy. Your future customers might read these reviews to decide if they want to visit your store or use your service. And when you respond to reviews? That shows you care. You're listening and you value feedback. People like that. They like feeling heard.

Let's not forget about the features that Google keeps adding. They're making this tool better all the time. You can now chat with customers directly from your profile. You can answer their questions, and they can even book appointments. It's like having a little assistant right there on Google, helping people connect with your business.

Now, you might be thinking, "How do I get started?" First, you'll want to claim your business on Google. It's as simple as telling Google, "Hey, this is my business!" Then you verify it, usually with a phone call or a postcard in the mail. Once that's done, you can start filling out all the details. The more you share, the better. It's like giving Google a map to your front door, so they can lead people right to you.

But it's not just a one-time deal. You keep your profile fresh by adding new photos, changing your hours if they shift, and posting updates. Just like you'd keep your store window looking nice to attract people passing by, you keep your Google Business Profile looking nice to attract people searching online.

Why is all this so important? Because in today's world, if you're not online, you're invisible to a whole lot of potential customers. Your Google Business Profile is your online storefront. It's where people look first to learn about you. And for local businesses, it might be the most important tool you have to bring people in the door.

So, take the time to make it shine. Use clear, easy language in your description. Share pictures that make people want to visit. Respond to reviews with kindness and thankfulness. Keep your information up to date. All these steps are simple, but they make a huge difference.

And remember, you're not alone in this. There are guides, like this one, that walk you through each step. You can take it slow, one bit at a time. You don't have to do it all in one day. But start today. Take one step. Maybe that's claiming your business. Maybe it's uploading a new photo. Just start.

By taking these steps, you're opening the door to your local customers. You're showing up where they're looking. And that's the first step to local domination. You're making your business easy to find and easy to choose. And that's what it's all about.

It's a powerful tool. And it's waiting for you to use it. So go ahead. Start today. Make your Google Business Profile the best it can be. It's your ticket to standing out in your local area. And we're here to help you every step of the way.

Optimizing Your GBP Listing

Think about a shop window. Now, imagine your business is behind that glass. People walk by and glance inside. What do they see? The answer to this question matters a lot when talking about your Google Business Profile (GBP). This profile is like your shop window on the internet, where people passing by are potential customers searching online. A well-dressed window grabs attention, right? Well, that's what we're aiming for with your GBP listing.

Let's start at the beginning. When you create your listing, you fill in information. This info tells people what you do, where you are, and how they can get in touch. Fill in every bit of it. Think of it as telling a new friend about your favorite place. You'd give them all the details, wouldn't you? Do the same here. Every detail counts.

Select categories for your business with care. Categories on GBP are like sections in a library. They guide people to your 'book' on the shelf. The main category should say exactly what you are. If you fix cars, your main category is 'auto repair shop.' Simple. You can add more categories, too. They can tell more about what you offer, like 'oil change service' or 'tire shop.'

Now, let's craft your description. This is where you tell your story. Keep it short and sweet. Explain what you offer, what makes you special, and why customers should choose you. Use words that feel warm and welcoming. Imagine you're inviting someone to your birthday party. You'd want them to feel excited to come, right? That's the feeling you want here.

Next up, photos. Photos can say a lot without words. They show what words can't. Take clear, bright pictures. Show your team, your products, and your place. Change them sometimes, like how shops change their window displays. It keeps things fresh and interesting. And people like that.

Remember, your GBP listing is like a handshake. It's the first meeting between you and your customers. Make it a firm, friendly, and memorable one. This way, you're not just another face in the crowd. You're the friendly local business that everyone wants to visit.

The steps we've talked about are simple, but they're powerful. Take your time with each one. Picture your business through the eyes of a customer and give them what they would want to see. If you do, you'll stand out in the best possible way. And that's just what we want, isn't it?

Engaging with Customers on GBP

Engaging with customers is one of the key steps to success for any service-based business. Especially when we talk about your Google Business Profile, or GBP. This is your stage, your platform to connect with your local customers. Think of GBP as a bridge. It connects you to people who are searching for the services you provide. And when these local customers find you, they might have things to say. They might ask questions or leave reviews about the service they received. How you respond to them can make a big difference.

Now, let's break it down, step by step, about how you can use GBP to engage with customers and build a relationship based on trust.

The first part of customer engagement on GBP is all about reviews. People often leave reviews after they have used your service. These can be good or bad. But every review is a chance for you to shine. Say someone leaves a nice comment saying they loved your service. You should thank them! Just a simple 'Thank you' can show that you care. It makes the person who wrote the review feel good, too. It's like giving them a smile after they said something nice about you. And other people will see this and think, 'Hey, this business cares about its customers.'

But what if someone leaves a bad review? It happens, but it's not the end of the world. In fact, it's another chance for you to show how awesome you are. Reply to them, too. In your reply, be kind. Say you are sorry they did not have a good experience. Tell them you want to make things better. Offer to talk with them to fix the problem. This shows everyone that you care about making things right. It's like if a friend tells you they are sad, and you say, 'I'm here for you.' It makes a difference.

Now, you might wonder about questions. People can ask you anything on your GBP. They might want to know if you offer a certain service, or if you are open on holidays. When they ask, you should answer. Try to do it quickly, too. This shows that you are there, ready to help. It's like if someone raises their hand to ask a question in class. You wouldn't ignore them. No, you'd help them understand. That's what you should do with customer questions on GBP.

Next, let's talk about posts and offers. Your GBP lets you post updates, like if you have a new service or a special deal. Think about when you see a sign for a sale in a store window. It grabs your attention, right? That's what your posts on GBP can do. They can tell people, 'Look, we have something cool for you!' Offers work the same way. Maybe you have a discount on a service. Tell people about it on GBP. They will like hearing about good deals. It's like when you find a dollar on the ground. It feels good, and you want to tell others about your good luck.

To wrap it up, engaging with customers on GBP is about talking and listening. It's about showing you care and are there to help. Every review, question, post, and offer is a chance to build trust. And trust is like a big, warm blanket. It makes everyone feel safe and happy. When you have trust, people come to you. They tell their friends about you. And that's how you grow. So, use GBP to talk to your customers. Listen to what they have to say. And always be kind and helpful. That's how you engage with customers on GBP. That's how you build trust.

Remember, this is your chance to talk with people who might walk through your door tomorrow. Make every word count. Make every interaction matter. Make sure they know you are listening, you care, and you are ready to help. That's engaging with customers on GBP. And that's how you build a business that lasts.

Leveraging GBP Insights

When you run a service-based business, knowing what your customers want and how they find you is like having a map to treasure. Sometimes, finding that map is easier than you think. It's right there in your Google Business Profile (GBP). With GBP, you can see all sorts of helpful information. This is what we call insights. They tell you a lot about your customers. They show you what's working and what's not. Like a compass guiding a sailor, these insights can steer your business in the right direction.

First, let's talk about what GBP insights are. These are numbers and bits of information that Google collects for you. They show you how customers find your business listing on Google. You can see if they found you by searching for your business name directly. Or if they found you by looking for a type of service or product that you offer. This is super useful. It tells you how well-known your business is. Or if you need to work harder to get noticed for what you sell or do.

Then, there are things like where customers view your business on Google. It could be on Maps or on the regular search results. If more people see you on Maps, they might be close by and ready to visit. If they find you on search results, they might still be looking around. So you can think about ways to get them to come over.

Also, GBP insights show you what customers do after they find your listing. Do they visit your website? Do they call you? Or do they ask for directions to your place? This is golden information. It tells you what customers do when they're interested in what you offer. If they mostly visit your website, make sure it's good and helpful. If they call you a lot, be ready to answer the phone and be friendly and helpful. If they ask for directions, they might just walk into your business any minute. So, make sure everything is neat and ready for them.

Now, why are these insights so important? They help you see if you're doing a good job online. If a lot of people find you when they search for a service you offer, it means your GBP is working well. You're likely to get more customers this way. If not many people find you for what you do, you need to think about how to fix that. Maybe you need better words in your profile or better pictures. Whatever it is, the insights tell you, so you can act.

Understanding customer actions is also super important. Let's say you notice that not many people call your business after they find you on Google. You might want to look at your phone number. Is it right? Is it easy to find? Sometimes, small changes can make a big difference. And these insights help you decide what to change. This is how you make your business better and attract more customers.

Next, how do you use these insights to help your business? You check them regularly. Make it a habit, like checking the mailbox. When you get familiar with these insights, you start to see patterns. Maybe more people find you on weekends. So, maybe you need to be extra ready for customers on those days. Or maybe they find you when they search for something specific. You can use this information to make ads or offers that fit what they're looking for.

Also, keep an eye on how new changes affect your insights. Say you add new photos of your shop. Do more people visit your profile after that? If yes, maybe they like seeing what your place looks like. So keep those photos coming. Keep track of all the changes you make and how people react to them. This is how you learn what works best for your business.

GBP insights can also show you the power of your responses to reviews. If you start replying to reviews, do more people come to your business after that? It could be that they like to see that you care about what customers think. This is a sign to keep replying to reviews and showing that you're a business that listens. It's all about learning from what the insights tell you and using that to do better.

And remember, don't get scared by numbers or think it's too technical. It's really not. It's just like learning to read a new kind of report card. You see what's good and what needs work. Then, you use that knowledge to make your business shine. It's about taking small steps based on what the insights are showing you. This way, you can slowly build up your business and become the go-to place for what you offer in your local area.

Finally, keep looking for new patterns in your GBP insights as your business grows. Maybe over time, you notice that people start finding your business by your name more often than by what you offer. This is great! It means your business is getting famous. People know you and look for you by name. When this happens, you know you're on the right track.

So, take a good look at your GBP insights often. They're like a friend telling you what's happening with your customers. They help you understand your business better. And they give you clear steps on what to do next. They're a powerful tool to help you grow and do well in your local area.

Now, you know how to use your GBP insights to help your business. It's all about paying attention, learning from what you see, and then taking action. It's about making your business the best it can be for your customers. And when you do that, they'll keep coming back, and they'll tell their friends too. That's how you become a local favorite. Good luck with your business, and have fun getting to know your customers better with GBP insights!

Advanced GBP Features and Opportunities

Google Business Profile, or GBP for short, is like a toolbox for your local business. It full of handy tools that can help your business shine. Some of these tools are well-known. But there are others that are not used as much. These lesser-known tools are what can give you an edge over the competition. Let's dig into these tools and see how they can work for you.

First off, there is a tool called the booking button. This button is a small but powerful feature. It lets customers book appointments with you directly from your GBP. This is great because it makes it so easy for customers to reach out and use your services. And when things are easy, people are more likely to do them.

Next, let's talk about messaging. This is a way for customers to send you messages right from your GBP listing. Imagine someone is looking for a service you offer. They find your business online. Now, they want to ask a quick question. With messaging, they can do this super easily. It's like sending a text message to a friend. Simple, right?

Then, there are product listings. These let you show off what you have to offer. You can add pictures and prices for your products. This way, when people find your business, they can see what you sell without having to go to your website. It's like having a mini shop right in the search results. How convenient is that?

Now, you might be thinking, "Okay, these features sound good. But why are they so important?" Well, they're important because they help you stand out. They give people more ways to connect with your business. And the more ways people can connect with you, the better your chances of getting new customers.

But how do you get started with these features? It's not hard at all. Let's go step by step. For the booking button, you first need to set up an account with one of Google's partners that offers booking services. Once you have that, you can link it to your GBP. And just like that, people can start booking appointments with you.

For messaging, you need to turn it on in your GBP account. Then, you can start chatting with customers. You can answer their questions and help them right away. This is really good for making customers feel taken care of. They'll remember how helpful you were, and that's a big plus.

Adding product listings is just as simple. You go to your GBP dashboard and find the products section. Then, you can add new products one by one. You can write a description, set a price, and upload a photo. This is your chance to show what makes your products special. So take the time to make these listings good.

But here's something very important. Google often adds new features to GBP. To really make the most of GBP, you need to stay up to date. You need to know when new tools come out. Then, you can be one of the first to use them. This can put you ahead of others who might not even know these tools exist.

So, how do you stay updated? You can check the Google Business Profile blog. You can also join forums or groups where people talk about GBP. This way, you'll hear about new features as soon as they're out. And then, you can jump right in and start using them. Staying informed is key to making GBP work its best for you.

Remember, using these advanced features is all about giving customers what they need. When you make things easy for them, they're more likely to choose your business. And when you offer them tools that other businesses don't, you really stand out. It's all about being helpful and being different. That's how you can use GBP to its full potential.

So, take some time today to look at your GBP. Are you using all the tools it offers? If not, now's the time to start. Add that booking button. Turn on messaging. Show off your products. And always keep an eye out for new features. This is how you can use GBP to make a big splash in your local market. And that's what it's all about, right? Making your business the go-to place for customers in your area.

In conclusion, while the basics of GBP are essential, it's these advanced features that can really give you an advantage. Start experimenting with them today. See what works for you. And keep learning about new opportunities as they come. With a little bit of effort, you'll not only be reaching more customers, but you'll also be offering them a better experience. And that's something that will definitely help your business grow.

Recap: Google Business Profile Mastery

You've been with us through the journey of understanding the Google Business Profile (GBP). Now, as we draw this chapter to a close, let's gather up the key pieces. They fit together like a puzzle, each one crucial to the full picture of dominating your local market. We will walk through a summary of strategies and an action checklist. By the end, you'll have a clear map to guide you on the path to GBP mastery.

A well-optimized GBP can help your service-based business shine in local searches. It's like a beacon, drawing nearby customers to your doorstep. This is why we took the time to explore every feature, every strategy, every opportunity that GBP offers.

But let's not just breeze by. Let's take a moment to really soak it in.

Remember the essentials we talked about? They are the foundation. GBP is not just a tool; it's a bridge. It connects you with your local community, with the people who are looking for exactly what you offer.

When you first create your GBP listing, you're setting the stage. You're telling the world, "Here I am, and here's what I can do for you." You choose categories carefully, choose words that describe your business in a welcoming way, and you add pictures that catch the eye. It's like setting up your shop window. But instead of a street, it's on the internet, where everyone can find you anytime.

Then, we discussed how to talk to your customers using GBP. Answer their reviews. Answer their questions. Let them know they matter. It's all about building trust and making connections. When you post updates or share special offers, it's like you're waving at passersby, inviting them in for a chat and maybe a cup of coffee.

Insights from GBP are like a secret map treasure hunters use. They tell you stories about who's searching for you, how they found you, and what they do once they see your business online. If you read this map right, it can guide you to make your business even better.

And don't forget those advanced features we covered. They are like hidden paths not many people know about. They can give you a shortcut to more visibility and better customer service. Things like having a button on your profile that lets people book your services right away, or being able to chat with them directly through GBP. It's about staying ahead, always moving, always improving.

Alright, are you ready? Here's your action checklist. Follow these steps, and you're on your way to making the most of your Google Business Profile:

- **Review the Basics:** Make sure your business information is accurate and up-to-date. This includes your name, address, phone number, and operating hours.

- **Enhance Your Description:** Craft a business description that's clear, inviting, and tells your unique story.
- **Add High-Quality Photos:** Choose images that showcase your business in the best light and attract attention.
- **Select the Right Categories:** Pick categories that accurately represent your business and help you show up for the right searches.
- **Respond to Reviews:** Take the time to reply to reviews, both positive and negative, to show that you value customer feedback.
- **Use Posts to Your Advantage:** Share updates, offers, and news about your business regularly to keep your GBP listing fresh.
- **Analyze Your Insights:** Look at your GBP analytics regularly to understand how customers find and interact with your listing.
- **Explore Advanced Features:** Try out additional features like messaging, booking buttons, and product listings to enhance customer interaction.
- **Stay Updated:** Keep an eye on new features and updates from GBP to ensure you're using the platform to its fullest potential.

By ticking off these items, you're not just checking boxes. You're building a foundation. You're creating a space where your local customers can find and connect with you easily. You're ensuring that when someone searches for a service you offer, it's your name they see, your business they choose, and your service they remember.

This is not the end. It's a new beginning. A journey that continues as you grow your presence, refine your approach, and ultimately, dominate your local market. So take a deep breath, roll up your sleeves, and let's make your business the local star it deserves to be.

Enhancing Visibility with Citations and Directories

The Impact of Citations on Local SEO

Citations are like friends who tell others where you live. They are little pieces of information that float around on the internet. These friends say, "This is where this business is. This is their phone number. This is their name." Each time they do this, they help people find your business.

Why does this matter? Let's break it down into small bits you can really use.

When you have a business, you want to make sure people can find you. Think of the internet like a huge city. In this city, you want your business to be easy to find, like a big, bright shop on the main street. Citations help by being signposts that point to your shop—the more signposts, the better. This is because search engines, like Google, look for these signposts. They want to see how many there are and if they all say the same thing.

Now, what makes up a citation? It has a few parts. There's your business name, which is like your name. It's how people know who you are. Then there's your address. This is like telling people where your house is. And there's your phone number, which is how people can talk to you. When all these parts are out there on the internet, they need to be the same everywhere. If they are not the same, it's like giving someone the wrong directions to your house. That's not good, right?

There are different types of citations too. Some are just the basic stuff, like your name, address, and phone number. Others give more details, like what your business does, or even pictures. The more details, the better. It's like telling a story about your business. People like stories. They remember stories. So, when you have a good citation that tells a good story, people remember your business.

In the end, what you want are good friends—no, great friends! Friends that tell the same story about your business. The better the story, the more people will come. And they need to keep telling that story. Over and over, in the same way, so everyone knows your business and can find it easily. That's how citations help you get seen in this big internet city.

So, to sum it all up, citations are super important. They help people find your business. They make sure the story of your business is out there. And they make sure the story is the same everywhere. This means more people walking into your shop, calling you, and buying from you.

Let me give you clear steps to make this work for you. First, go and see what the internet says about your business. Check if your business name, address, and phone number are the same everywhere. If they're not, write down where they're wrong. Then, one by one, fix them. Make them all match. This is something you can do today. And it will help people find you more easily tomorrow.

Remember, having a great business is like having a treasure. But it's not very useful if no one can find it. Citations are your map. Make sure your map is clear and the same everywhere. This way, everyone can find your treasure—your business.

Selecting the Right Directories and Platforms

When you have a service-based business, getting noticed by local clients is like finding treasure. It's valuable. To do this, you need to be in the right places where people are looking. This is where directories and platforms come into play. Think of directories as big signs that point to your business. But not all signs are the same. Some are shiny and big, and others are small and hard to see. You need the shiny, big ones. So, let's talk about choosing the best directories that are like the big, shiny signs for your business.

First, you want to look at directories that are all about your kind of work. If you fix cars, you want to be listed where people look for car repair. This is what we call directory relevance. It makes no sense to be listed in a place where people look for something else. It's a waste of time, and you won't get the clients you want. To find these right places, you can start with a simple web search. Look up where your competitors are listed. You can also ask your customers where they found you. This gives you a clue about where people look for your services.

Now, think about quality over quantity. It's better to have your business in a few good places than in many not-so-good ones. A good directory is like a good friend. It's trustworthy and has a good name. If you're seen with it, people think well of you. A bad directory is like a friend who is always in trouble. You don't want to be seen with them because it looks bad for you. So, choose directories that are respected and have a lot of people using them. They should look nice and be easy for people to use. Check if they show up on the first page of search results. That's a good sign.

There are also what we call niche directories. These are special places for specific kinds of businesses. Like clubs for people with special interests. If you find one for your type of service, it's a big win. Being listed there is like being in a VIP area. It's exclusive and it tells clients you are a perfect fit for what they need. To find these niche directories, you can look for groups or associations related to your business. They often have directories. You can

74

also look for online communities that talk about the services you offer. They might know the secret places where your ideal clients hang out.

So, here's what you can do right now. Sit down with your computer or phone. Start searching for directories and platforms that match your business. Make a list. Check each one to see if it's a good fit. Look at how they look, what they offer, and if they're on the first page of search results. Then pick the best ones and get your business on them. It's like setting up signs that point right to your door. And when you do it right, people will follow those signs and find their way to you. It's that simple. And it's something you can start doing today. Go on, get noticed and bring those local clients to your doorstep!

Crafting Consistent Citation Profiles

Let's dive into a world where every detail about your business online matches up. It sounds simple, right? Well, it is crucial. Imagine you find your favorite pizza place online. But, oops, the phone number is wrong. That's a problem. This is where consistent citation profiles come in.

First off, what is a citation? Think of it as a shout-out for your business on the internet. It could be on a directory, a social media page, or a local business listing. The key parts of this shout-out are your business name, address, and phone number. Together, they are often called NAP. Keep them the same everywhere. That's right, everywhere!

Why does this matter? Search engines like Google look at these shout-outs. They check if your business is real and reliable. And when they see the same details everywhere, they trust you more. This trust can make your business climb up in search results. And that means more people can find you when they search for what you offer.

So, let's focus on how to craft your citation profiles. Start with your

NAP. It needs to be the same in each place. The same name, the same address, the same phone number. If you're called "Sam's Delicious Pizza," don't be "Sam's Pizza" somewhere else. Details matter.

Next, think about your business description. This tells people what you do. Keep it simple. Make it clear. Tell them about the mouth-watering pizza you make. Mention your quick delivery. Share about your fresh, local ingredients. This is your chance to shine and make a mark in their minds.

But wait, there's more. Use pictures and videos too. Show off that golden crust. Let them see your chefs tossing dough in the air. Videos of happy customers biting into a slice? Perfect. These images catch the eye. They make people stop scrolling and pay attention to you.

Remember, your citations are not just information. They are your online voice. They talk to your customers even when you're not there. They can bring people through your door. So, take the time to craft them well. Pay attention to every word. Keep your NAP consistent. Make your business description inviting. And use visuals to tell your story.

When you get this right, you build trust. You show up better in search results. And those search results can turn into phone calls, visits, and sales. That's what you want, isn't it?

In the end, it's all about being found by the right people at the right time. And that starts with crafting consistent citation profiles. Let's do it well. Let's get noticed. Let's get those customers coming in.

Monitoring and Updating Citations

Keeping an eye on your business's online citations is like making sure all the lights on your car's dashboard are working right. Both tell you important things. For your car, it's about oil and gas. For your business, it's about being easy to find online. Now, let's talk about the best ways to keep track of your citations and keep them up to date.

The tools for watching over your citations come in all shapes and sizes. Some are simple and free. Others cost money but do more things. Think of these tools as helpers that do the hard work of looking all over the internet to find where your business is listed. They check if your business name, address, and phone number, which folks call NAP, are the same everywhere. They tell you if something is wrong. This is super important. Why? Because if your NAP info is wrong somewhere, it can confuse both people and computers. And when computers get confused, they might not show your business in search results. And we don't want that.

Once you pick a good tool, it'll help you see where your business shows up online. But that's only the start. You also need to roll up your sleeves and make sure all your info is up-to-date. This means checking in on your listings from time to time. Think of it like watering plants. You don't do it once and forget it. You keep coming back to give them what they need to grow. Your business listings need the same kind of care.

But wait, a question pops up. How often should you update your citations? Well, you should check them whenever something changes. Like if you move to a new place, get a new phone number, or change your hours of opening. And even if nothing changes, it's a good idea to check them every few months. Just to be sure everything's still A-okay.

What if you find a mistake? What if you find two listings for your business that say different things? You need to fix this. It's like finding two different signs pointing to your house. People will get lost. So, when you find a mistake or a duplicate listing, you talk to the website where you found it. Tell them nicely, "Hey, this info is not right. Can you change it?" They'll usually help you out. If they don't, keep trying. It's that important.

Remember, all this keeping track and updating stuff matters a whole lot. When your business info is the same everywhere, it makes you look good. It shows you pay attention to the little things. And it helps people and computers trust you. That means more people can find you. And that means more people can walk into your shop, or call you, or send you an email asking for your services.

So, in short, here's what you need to do. Find a good tool to watch over your citations. Use it to make sure your NAP info is the same everywhere. Update your info whenever something changes. Check your listings every few months, even if nothing changes. Fix mistakes or duplicates right away. Do all this, and your business will be easier to find. That's what we want. We want people to find you, walk in your door, and become your customers. And by taking care of your online info, you help make that happen.

Overcoming Common Citation Challenges

Okay, so we have our business. We want people to find us, right? Here's the thing: citations can either help a lot or hurt a lot. Let's talk about how to fix them when they go wrong. Citations are like signposts on the internet that tell people where we are. But sometimes, they get messy.

First off, what if information about our business is different all over the web? That's a big no-no. Imagine someone trying to call you but the number is wrong. Frustrating, right? Here's what you do: You go on a search mission. Find all the places where your business is listed. Look at them closely. Is the address the same everywhere? How about the phone number? Don't forget the website link. These all have to match up.

Now, suppose you find mistakes. You'll need to fix them. How? Reach out to the website where the wrong info is. Ask them nicely to update it. Yes, it takes time. But think about it: every correct citation is a chance for a new customer to find you. Totally worth it, right?

Next up, let's talk about spammy citations. Not the canned meat, but the bad kind for your business. These are fake or low-quality listings that can pop up. They're not your friend. They can confuse people and mess with search engines. So, what to do? Clean up time. Find them and ask the website to take them down. Some websites might not listen. But keep trying. Getting rid of spammy citations helps clean up your business's online image.

Lastly, we've got businesses with lots of locations or a big pile of listings. Keeping track of all those citations? Big job. But here's a secret: you don't have to do it alone. There are tools out there that can help. They keep an eye on your citations for you. They'll tell you if something changes or if there's a mistake. It's like having a helper who's always watching out for your business's good name.

Remember, folks, accurate citations make it easy for customers to find you. They tell search engines, "Hey, this business is legit." And you want that, because being easy to find means more customers walking through your door. Keep those citations clean and correct, and watch your local business grow. It's all about being present and correct in the online world. Easy, right?

So, to wrap it up: hunt down your citations, make sure they're all saying the right thing, kick spammy ones to the curb, and use smart tools if you've got a big business to watch over. Do this, and you'll be smiling every time someone says, "I found you online, and I'm glad I did!"

There you go. Step by step, you can make sure your business shines online. It's not just about being out there. It's about being out there in the right way. That's how you win with citations. And that's how you'll make it easier for customers to come knocking. Now, take these steps, put them into action, and let's make your business the talk of the town.

Recap: Citations as a Local SEO Tool

So, you've just gone through a mountain of insights about citations and directories. It's a lot to take in, right? But hang in there. We're about to wrap it all up in a neat bow. This is where we bring it all together so you can step out into the world and make these tools work for your service-based business. You're going to see just how powerful simple steps can be when boosting your local SEO.

First, let's talk about why we've been harping on about citations and directories. They're not just online spots to slap your business name; they're way more than that. Citations and directories are like digital signposts that point potential clients right to your doorstep. They tell search engines, "Hey, this business is legit, and it's right here!" That's why they're so important for your local SEO.

Now, remember the core elements of a citation? That's your business name, address, and phone number, also known as NAP. These tidbits of info must be accurate wherever they appear. Search engines are smart, but they can get confused by inconsistent details. And trust me, you don't want to confuse them. A confused search engine could mean a drop in your rankings, and we can't have that.

It's also worth revisiting the types of directories and platforms out there. Not all directories are created equal. You want to aim for those that are relevant to your business. Think of it as choosing the right party to attend. You don't want to be the clown at a black-tie event, right? So, pick directories that fit your business vibe and are frequented by your potential clients.

Now, let's jog your memory on the maintenance side of things.

Keeping track of your citations is like keeping your garden free of weeds. You've got to check in on them, make sure they're still accurate, and update them when things change. Change of address? New phone number? Make those updates a priority.

And just when you think you've got it all down, you might run into some common roadblocks. Inconsistent information, citation spam, and managing multiple locations are just a few. But don't sweat it. With the right strategies, you can overcome these challenges and keep your citations clean and effective.

Feeling overwhelmed? I've got your back. Here's an actionable checklist for you to tackle your citations and directory listings. It's a step-by-step guide to keep things as easy as pie.

- **Verify Your NAP:** Make sure your business name, address, and phone number are the same across all listings.
- **Choose Quality Directories:** List your business on platforms that line up with your service and client base.
- **Update Regularly:** Keep your information fresh and accurate. Changes in your business details? Update immediately.
- **Multimedia is Your Friend:** Add photos and videos to your listings to grab attention and show off your business.
- **Monitor Your Online Presence:** Use tools to keep an eye on your citations and make fixes as needed.
- **Address Inconsistencies:** Spot a mistake? Correct it fast to keep search engines and clients on the right track.
- **Deal with Spam:** Watch out for spammy citations and get them removed to protect your SEO.
- **Scale Your Efforts:** If you have multiple locations, find a system to manage citations for all your spots.

There you have it. A simple, no-frills plan to take your local SEO to the next level with citations and directories. It's not magic. It's about being smart, paying attention, and staying on top of your game. Now it's time for you to get out there and make these steps work for your business.

You now have the knowledge and tools to master your online presence and boost your local visibility. Remember, it's not just about the information you've learned; it's about taking action. So, take this checklist, roll up your sleeves, and dive in. Your business will thank you for it.

One last thing before you go. This isn't a one-and-done deal. Keep this guide handy, revisit it often, and keep refining your approach. The world of SEO is always shifting, and your business needs to dance to the beat. Stay proactive, stay visible, and watch your local market presence grow.

So, take a deep breath, grab your digital tools, and tackle those citations and directories with confidence. You've got this!

Building a Strong Online Reputation

The Value of Online Reviews

Online reviews are like gold for a service-based business. Think about the last time you wanted to try a new restaurant or hire someone to fix your roof. What did you do first? You probably went online to see what other people said about them. That's what most of us do these days. We look for those stars next to a business name. We read what others say about their experiences. And it matters. It really does.

When people say good things about a business, it's like a signal to others that this place or service is worth their time. It's like seeing a long line outside a food truck. It makes you think, "That food must be delicious." It's the same with online reviews. Lots of good reviews can mean that a business gives great service or has the best products. And that's important. It makes people feel more sure about choosing that business.

But reviews do more than just make a business look good. They also help a business show up in online searches. Yes, that's right. When a business gets more good reviews, it can move up in search results. This means when you look for a plumber in your town, the one with lots of positive reviews might show up first. And that means more eyes on that business. More potential customers finding them without having to scroll down too much.

Let's talk more about why reviews matter so much. They give a business what we call credibility. Credibility is a big word that means trust. If you can trust a business to do what it says, that's credibility. And reliability is like a promise. When a business is reliable, it means you can count on them to do a good job every time. Good reviews tell us that a business is both credible and reliable. And that's the kind of business we all want to find.

So, if you're a business owner, you want to get as many good reviews as you can. It's one of the most important things you can do online. It's like making sure your shop sign is bright and easy to see. Good reviews draw people in. They make them think, "This must be the place to go." And once they think that, they're more likely to pick you over someone else.

Now, you might be wondering how to get these reviews. It's pretty simple, really. Do a great job. Make your customers happy. And then, just ask them. Ask them to share their happy thoughts online. It's okay to do that. Most people don't mind leaving a review if they had a good experience. Especially if you make it easy for them. Like sending a thank you email with a link to where they can leave their review. Keep it simple and easy, and many will be happy to help out.

Remember, each review is a little story about your business. A story told by someone else. And we all know that when someone else tells a good story about us, it can be powerful. More powerful than if we say it ourselves. That's the magic of reviews. They're stories that can help your business grow. And the more good stories you have out there, the better it is for you.

Managing and Responding to Reviews

When it comes to handling reviews, let's think about this. You have a business that you're proud of. You've put in the work and sweat to build it. And now, you get feedback in the form of reviews. Guess what? This feedback is a treasure trove. It's your chance to shine, to show how much you care, and to grow even more. Now, how do you make sure that you manage and respond to reviews in a way that helps your business thrive? Let's take it one step at a time.

First, you've got to keep an eye on what people are saying about you. This means watching different websites, like Google, Yelp, and Facebook. Imagine a person speaking about your business on one of these sites. That's a voice you want to hear. Why? Because it tells you how you're doing and what you can do better. Plus, other people read these words too. They learn from them before they even meet you.

Let's say you find a review. It's a good one. Someone is happy with your work. What do you do? You say thank you. You do it promptly and warmly. Let them know you appreciate their words. It's like if a friend complimented your cooking. You'd smile and thank them, right? This is the same. It's polite and it tells others you're a class act.

But what if a review isn't so sunny? It happens. Nobody's perfect, and sometimes things slip. This is your chance to show real character. You respond, but how? You stay kind and calm. You say you're sorry they're not happy. You're honest and ask how you can make things right. It's just like if you stepped on someone's toe. You didn't mean to, but you'd still say sorry and see if they're okay.

You might wonder why you would admit a mistake for everyone to see. Here's the thing. It shows you're human. It shows you care. And that matters to people. They see a business that doesn't run and hide. Instead, it stands up and wants to do better. That builds trust. And trust is key to making your business one that people want to come back to.

Here's something else to remember. When you write back to a review, do it like you're talking to the person face-to-face. Be nice. Be respectful. It's like you're having a chat over a cup of tea. You wouldn't shout or be mean, would you? Of course not. That's not how you build a good relationship. So, you write in a way that's friendly and helpful.

Now, you might get busy. Reviews come in, and it's tough to keep up. This is where setting aside time helps. Maybe you pick a time each day or week for review duty. You sit down, read what's new and write back. It's like having a set time for checking your mail. It keeps you from missing anything important.

Here's a tip. When you write back to someone, use their name. It makes your response personal and special. Think of it like getting mail with your name on it instead of "To the Resident." Which one feels better? The one with your name, right? That's what using their name in your response does. It makes the person feel seen and valued.

If you're scratching your head thinking, "That's a lot to keep track of," you're right. But there's help. You can use tools made just for this. They can tell you when you get a new review. This way, you can jump right in and respond. It's like having a good friend who nudges you and says, "Hey, someone's talking about you."

Let's wrap this up with a clear picture. Managing and responding to reviews is about being on top of what's said about your business. It's about saying thank you when people are happy and fixing things when they're not. It's about being respectful and showing you really listen. When you do this, people notice. They see a business that's got its heart in the right place. And that's the kind of business people like and trust. That's the kind of business they tell their friends about and keep coming back to.

So, take these words and put them into action. Watch for new reviews. Say thank you. Be kind and fix what's wrong. Use names and be respectful. Set time aside for this important task. And maybe get a tool that helps. Do this, and you'll build a reputation as a business that really cares about its customers. And that's a reputation that can take you far.

Encouraging Customer Reviews

Getting customers to leave reviews is like planting a garden. You need the right seeds, a bit of nurturing, and patience. Now, let's talk about planting these 'review seeds' right.

First things first, we need to play by the rules. Every review platform has them, and we must follow suit. No bribes. No fake reviews. We keep it honest, and we keep it clean. That's non-negotiable.

So, how do we get those reviews rolling in? It starts with asking. But not just any kind of asking. You want to make it part of your service. After you've done something great for your customer, that's your moment. Say something like, "Hey, I'm thrilled you're happy with our service. It would mean the world to us if you could share your experience with others." It's sincere. It's direct. And it shows you value their opinion.

Now, let's make it easy for them. Ever tried to do something online and given up because it was too hard? We don't want that. We want to make leaving a review as easy as pie. So, give them a link. Direct them right to where they can spill their happy thoughts. No searching, no guessing. Just a simple click and they're there. But you might wonder, where do I send them? Well, think about where your customers hang out. Is it Google? Facebook? Choose the place that makes sense for your business and your customers.

Next, we've got timing. Timing is everything. Ask too soon, and they might not have fully enjoyed your service. Ask too late, they might not remember the specifics. Find that sweet spot. Maybe it's right after you've delivered your product or completed your service. When their satisfaction is fresh and their excitement is high, that's your cue.

Let's not forget our manners. Say thank you. Whether it's a glowing review or a not-so-shiny one, a simple thank you goes a long way. It shows you're listening and you care. And when you show that, customers are more likely to share.

But what about those who forget? We're all human. We get busy. A gentle nudge can work wonders. Send a friendly reminder. But keep it light. Something like, "Hey, just checking in to see if you had a moment to share your thoughts on our service. It helps us a lot!" Remember, we're not pushing; we're just giving a little tap on the shoulder.

Here's a tip. Make it a part of your process. Like clockwork. Every time you wrap up a service, you know the next tick is to encourage a review. Build it into your routine. That way, you won't forget, and your customers will sense it's a normal part of your excellent service.

Now, let's talk about incentives. But remember, we're not breaking rules. We're not saying, "Give us a good review, and we'll give you a gift." No. Instead, we're making it about appreciation. You could have a monthly draw. Every customer who leaves a review enters to win something neat. It's random. It's fun. And it's completely within the rules.

Lastly, let's keep an eye on the long game. Building a strong reputation with lots of good reviews doesn't happen overnight. It's a marathon, not a sprint. Keep at it. Keep refining your approach. And keep listening to your customers. They're the ones who will help you grow and succeed.

So there you go. That's how you encourage customer reviews. It's about asking nicely, making it a breeze, and showing your gratitude. It's about being patient and consistent. And it's about staying genuine and playing fair. Do these things, and you'll see your garden of reviews start to bloom.

And when it does, that's when the magic happens. More reviews mean more trust. And more trust means more customers. It's a beautiful cycle, one that starts with a simple seed. Your service.

Leveraging Testimonials and Case Studies

Ever noticed how a good story sticks with you? When a friend tells you about their experience at a new restaurant or how they felt using a new gadget, you listen. You get curious. Sometimes, you even act on their recommendation. This is the secret sauce of using testimonials and case studies for your business. Let's talk about how you can use these powerful tools to show off your successes and win over new clients.

First things first, what are testimonials? They are those sweet, short stories customers tell about how your service made their day, solved a problem, or just gave them a smile. They're like personal shout-outs of satisfaction. Now, case studies are a bit like testimonials. But think of them as the bigger sibling. A case study goes deeper. It tells a tale of a challenge faced, the solutions given, and the happy ending achieved.

Why are these important? Well, people trust other people. When they hear someone else got great results, they think they might too. It's like when a friend says, "Hey, I tried this and it worked for me!" You believe them because you know they wouldn't steer you wrong. That trust is gold for your business.

So, let's dive into how you can gather these golden nuggets of praise. When your service knocks it out of the park, often a customer will tell you right then and there. That's your cue. Ask them if they'd mind sharing their thoughts in writing. Most happy customers will say yes. After all, who doesn't like to spread a bit of joy?

Now you've got a testimonial. Great! But don't just leave it in an email or a thank you card. Put it out there where future customers can see it. Your website is a good home for it. So is your social media. Think about where your customers hang out online. That's where you want these stories to be.

But remember, keep it real. Only use words your customers said. It's tempting to spice things up, but honesty is what builds trust. And trust is what you're after, right?

Now let's get to case studies. These take more work, but boy, are they worth it. You need to set the stage. Tell us what the problem was. Then walk us through how you tackled it. End with the win – the results. It's like a mini adventure where you're the hero.

Creating a case study can be fun. You get to play storyteller. Gather the facts, maybe some before-and-after pictures, or data showing improvements. Lay it out like a story with a beginning, middle, and end. Make it something that grabs attention, something that pulls people in. And just like testimonials, put your case studies where they can shine. Your website is perfect for this. A blog or a special page that says, "Look at what we can do!"

But wait, there's more to it. You want these stories to not just be seen, but to be felt. That's where the art of storytelling comes in. You want to make it so that when someone reads your case study, they can see themselves in it. They start thinking, "Hey, that could be me!"

So how do you do that? Keep it simple. Use words people use in everyday talk. No big, fancy words that make you grab a dictionary. Write like you're telling a friend about this awesome thing that happened. And just like chatting with a friend, keep it light, keep it interesting.

One more thing – update these stories. As your business grows, you'll have more stories to tell. Keep adding new testimonials and fresh case studies. They show you're always improving, always delivering good stuff. It's like showing off a scrapbook of wins. The more you have, the better it looks.

To wrap it up, remember how good stories stick with you? That's what you're aiming for. You want potential clients to read these testimonials and case studies and think, "I want that to be my story too." So get out there, collect those stories, and share them. They're not just praise. They're proof that what you do works. And that's something worth talking about.

Reputation Management Tools and Practices

Building a strong online presence is like taking care of a garden. You plant the seeds of your service and tend to them daily. Reputation management tools are the watering cans and gardening gloves that help your online garden thrive. They are the helpers that allow you to know what others say about your business. Let's dig into these tools and practices one by one.

In today's world, where people look online before they buy almost anything, what they find can make a big difference. Think about how you search for a restaurant or a mechanic. You look them up online, right? You read what other people say. Now, imagine people doing the same for your business. That's where reputation management tools come in handy.

Reputation management software is like a big, friendly dog that barks whenever someone comes to your gate. It lets you know when someone leaves a review or talks about your service online. With so much happening on the internet, it's tough to keep an eye on everything by yourself. That's why these tools are so useful. They track what's said about your service on review sites, social media, and more. When there's a new review or comment, these tools tell you right away. This means you can say thank you for a nice review or quickly fix a problem if someone wasn't happy.

But it's not just about knowing what people say. It's also about talking back. When you reply to reviews, both good and bad, you show you care.

Good replies make happy customers even happier. They make them want to come back. And when you reply well to a bad review, it can turn a sad customer into a happy one. It can also show other people reading the review that you're a good person to do business with.

Now, let's take a moment to think about being proactive. It's like putting up a strong fence so that fewer things go wrong in your garden. A proactive approach means asking for feedback before customers even leave your place. It's about making everything so good from the start that people want to say nice things about you. It's also about fixing small problems before they turn into big ones that people talk about online.

There are different kinds of reputation management tools. Some are simple and look only at reviews. Others are more complex and can look at social media, news, and more. Prices also vary. Some tools are free, but others cost money. It's important to find the right one for your business. Think about how big your business is and where your customers like to talk. That's how you'll know which tool is best for you.

Here's an idea for you. Set up a system where you check your online reviews once a day or once a week. Pick a day and time. Make it a habit. When you do this, you always know what's happening. And if a tool sends you an alert, you can look right away. This shows customers that you're always there, always listening, and always ready to make things right. It's a way to build trust and make sure people have good things to say about you.

Let's talk about something else that's really important: What you say when you reply to reviews. Always be kind and professional. Even if the review is mean or unfair, answer nicely. Other people will see this and know you're someone who cares. If the review is about a problem, say you're sorry and tell how you can fix it. If the review is good, say thank you and maybe invite the person back. It's simple, but it makes a big difference.

To wrap things up, remember that managing your online reputation is just as important as the service you provide. Tools can help a lot, but they're just tools. It's how you use them that counts. Keep your replies kind and helpful. Always be ready to make things right. And use these tools to be aware of what others say. If you do these things, your online garden will grow to be beautiful and full of happy customers. Plus, you'll stand out from others who may not take such good care of their garden.

So, step up and start nurturing your online reputation today. It's a powerful way to keep your service growing strong and your customers coming back for more.

Recap: The Pillars of Online Reputation

Building a strong online reputation is like planting a garden. It takes time, patience, and the right tools to grow. In the world of service-based businesses, your online reputation is often the first thing potential customers see. It's what they use to judge if they can trust you. And just like a garden, if you care for it well, it will flourish and bring you lots of good things. We've learned a lot about online reputation in this chapter. Let's take a moment to go over the main points.

First, we talked about online reviews. We learned that these reviews are super important. They're not just comments; they're powerful signals to other people that say, "Hey, this business is worth your time!" or "Hmm, maybe think twice." Reviews can also help your business show up when people search for services like yours on the internet. This is a part of what some folks call "local SEO." It's like telling search engines that your business is a big deal in your area.

Next, we learned how to keep an eye on what people are saying about us in their reviews. We saw how to answer them in a way that shows we care about our customers. Whether they say something nice or not so nice, it's our chance to show that we're listening. When you respond well, you tell everyone that your business is the kind of place that values its customers. This is huge for your image.

After that, we looked at ways to get more customers to leave reviews. We want to make it easy for them and make them feel like their opinion is really wanted. But we have to play by the rules. We can't give them something in return that's against the rules of the platform they're reviewing on. We have to be smart about it.

We also saw how stories from happy customers can make a big difference. Testimonials and case studies on your website can show off the great things your business has done. They're like little stories that say, "Look what we can do for you too!"

Then we learned about tools that can help us keep track of our online reputation. With the right software, this job can be a lot easier. It's like having a helper in your garden to tell you which plants need more water or which ones are doing great.

Now, let's get into the action. Here's a checklist for keeping your online reputation healthy and strong:

- Set up alerts to know when a new review comes in. You can use tools like Google Alerts for this.
- Check your reviews every day. It's like watering your garden – do it regularly!
- Respond to reviews, both good and bad, in a kind way. Say thank you to the happy customers. Offer help to the ones who weren't happy.
- Ask customers to leave a review. Maybe you can do this after they've used your service, with a friendly email or text.

- Share your best reviews on your website and social media. It's like showing off the best flowers in your garden.
- Use reputation management software to help you stay on top of things. It's like a toolshed stocked with everything you need for the garden.
- Make a plan for what to do if someone leaves a really bad review. It's like having a first aid kit ready, just in case.
- Keep improving your service. The better your service, the better the reviews you'll get. It's like using the best seeds for your garden.

Remember, your online reputation is always growing, just like a garden. You have to take care of it all the time. But if you do, it will reward you with trust from customers and a better spot in search results. That's what we all want, right? A thriving business that people love and trust.

So, take these steps and use them. Pay attention to your online reputation every day. It's a big part of your business's success. When you look after it, you're making sure that your business is as awesome online as it is in real life. And that's something to be proud of.

Content Marketing for Local Engagement

Content as a Local Engagement Driver

Content marketing is a powerful tool. It's like a magnet that attracts people to your business. But not just any people. We're talking about folks from your neighborhood, your city, your community. Think about your favorite local coffee shop. Now, how did you first learn about it? Maybe you read an article about the best coffee spots in town or saw a post on social media from a friend who was raving about their caramel macchiato. That's content marketing at work, reaching out to you, right where you live.

So, what makes content marketing so special for local businesses? It's personal. It's about creating a bond with your neighbors. When you share stories, news, and tips that matter to your local audience, you're tapping into their daily lives. You're no longer a faceless business. You become a trusted friend they can rely on. And friends support each other, don't they?

Building local brand awareness is crucial. It's making sure people know your business exists. It's like putting up a big, bright sign that says, "Hey, we're here, and we've got what you need!" But it's more than just getting noticed. It's about showing your community that you understand them. That you care about the same things they care about. Whether it's supporting local events or addressing local issues, your content says, "We're in this together."

Credibility is another piece of the puzzle. It's not enough for people to know you're there. They need to trust you. Trust comes from proving that you're reliable, that you know your stuff, and that you always put your customers first. How do you show that? Through thoughtful, helpful content. Maybe it's a blog post that helps them solve a common problem or a how-to video that makes their lives easier. When you give them value, they give you trust.

Now, you might be thinking, "Sounds great, but how do I even start?" Good question. It starts with knowing your audience. Who are they? What do they like? What do they need? Once you have that figured out, you can create content that speaks directly to them. It's like knowing your friend's favorite candy and surprising them with it. It shows you're paying attention.

Think about the last time you really helped a friend. How did it make you feel? Now, imagine doing that for your entire local community. Every piece of content you create is a chance to help someone, to make their day just a bit better. And when you do that consistently, you're not just a local business anymore. You become a local hero. Sounds good, right?

Now, this doesn't mean you need to spend a lot of money. No, it's about being smart. It's about finding ways to reach out to your local audience in a way that feels natural. Social media can be your best friend here. It's free, it's easy, and it's where your customers are hanging out. Posting pictures from recent events, sharing updates about your business, or offering special deals just for your followers—all of these are ways to engage with your community without breaking the bank.

Remember, content marketing isn't a one-time deal. It's not about making a single splash and then fading into the background. It's about creating a consistent, ongoing conversation with your local customers. It's about staying present in their minds, so when they need what you offer, you're the first name that pops up. And the best part? This kind of marketing gets stronger over time. The more you do it, the more your community will recognize and appreciate your efforts.

Let's recap what we've covered here:

- Content marketing connects you with your local community.
- It's about building brand awareness and trust by providing value.
- Understanding your local audience is key to creating relevant content.
- You don't need a big budget, just smart, consistent efforts.
- Engaging with your community strengthens your business over time.

So now you know why content marketing is like a secret weapon for local engagement. It's personal, it's powerful, and best of all, it's something you can start doing today. Go ahead, take the first step. Share a story, post a tip, offer advice. Be that friend to your community, and watch how they support you back. It's time to let your content do the talking.

Planning Your Content Strategy

When you have a local business, you want people nearby to come and visit. To get their attention, you have to tell them about your shop or service. This is where a good plan for your messages, or a content strategy, comes in. Think of it as a map that shows you how to talk to your neighbors and make them want to see what you offer.

A good content strategy starts with knowing what goals you want to reach. Maybe you want more people to visit your shop. Or you want them to like and trust your brand. Whatever your goals are, write them down. They will guide every message you send out.

Now, let's talk about why planning your messages is so important. You want to talk to people regularly. If you talk too much, they might get tired of hearing from you. But if you don't talk enough, they might forget you. You need to find a balance. This is why you need a content calendar. A calendar helps you plan when to talk to people. It makes sure you don't forget to send an important message. And it helps you keep track of what you've already told them.

A content calendar is like a planner for your business. It tells you what to say and when to say it. You can use a simple calendar on your computer or a big one on your wall. On this calendar, you will write down each message you want to send. You will also write down the date you want to send it. This keeps your message plan neat and organized.

When you make your calendar, think about special days. These might be holidays or events in your town. These are great times to talk to people because they are already in a good mood. You can share messages that match the holiday or event. This makes your brand feel friendly and connected to the community.

Also, think about the times when people might need your service more. If you fix heaters, people need you most when it's cold. So, plan to talk to them before it gets cold. Tell them how you can help them stay warm. If you sell school supplies, talk to families before school starts. They will be looking for the things you sell. A good plan helps you talk to the right people at the right time.

Remember, your messages can be many things. They can be a post on a website, a picture on social media, or even a sign in your store. They are all ways to tell people about your business. And they all should be part of your content calendar.

Think of each message as a tiny seed. Each seed has the chance to grow into a big tree. But it needs care. You need to plant it at the right time and give it what it needs to grow. This is why planning when and what to say is so important. It gives each message the best chance to make people want to visit your business.

Finally, keep your messages simple. Use words that everyone can understand. You want people to read your message and know right away how you can help them. If they have to think too hard about it, they might not pay attention. So, keep it clear and easy.

To wrap up, planning your content strategy is like planning a party. You need to know who you want to invite, what you want to happen, and when the party should be. A good plan makes sure the party is fun and everyone has a good time. For your business, a good plan makes sure your messages help people learn about you and make them want to stop by.

Now, it's time to grab that calendar and start planning your messages. Write down your goals, think about the best times to talk to people, and plan messages that are simple and friendly. This way, people in your town will get to know your brand. And they'll think of you when they need what you offer. That's how you make a good content strategy work for your local business.

Creating Locally Relevant Content

When you create content for a local audience, think about what makes your neighborhood special. Picture the streets, the stores, and the people. What makes your community unique? Your content should be like a friendly chat with your neighbor over the fence, sharing stories and news that matter right here, right now.

Let's start with understanding your local crowd. To engage them, you need to know what they like, what they talk about, and what problems they have that you can solve. It's all about them, not just what you have to offer. Keep this in mind as you pick up your pen or sit down at your keyboard.

Now, let's dive into some guidelines. Remember, your goal is to craft content that feels like it was made just for your local pals. You want them to read your words and think, "This is for me!"

First up, what's going on around town? Are there any events, holidays, or local heroes making waves? Use these as a springboard for your content. Maybe write about how your service can spice up a local festival or how it honors the hard work of community leaders.

Next, talk about local issues. Maybe there's a pothole epidemic or a new park opening up. How does your service fit into this picture? For example, if you're a landscaper, offer tips on how to make the most of that new park with a beautiful picnic setup.

Also, consider the language. Use words that are common in your area. If everyone calls a sub sandwich a "hoagie," then you should too. It's like wearing the home team's jersey – it shows you're one of them.

Let's get practical. List tips, how-tos, or even a step-by-step guide that solves a local problem, using plain language. Instead of saying, "Optimize your household waste disposal techniques," you'd say, "Here's how to sort your trash quick and easy for our town's recycling day."

Stories are powerful, too. Share tales of local customers who've had great experiences with your service. Just tell it straight – no need for fancy words. It's about making a connection, showing your neighbors how you've helped someone just like them.

Remember, images and videos can speak volumes. Capture the local scenery, the landmarks, or even the high school football team's big win. Then, connect it back to your service in a way that feels natural, like, "Our car wash is just down the street from where our team made history!"

Now, let's talk about the kinds of content you can create. Blog posts, social media updates, newsletters – these are all great. But tailor them to your town. A blog post could be about "The 5 Best Picnic Spots in [Your Town]." A social media update could showcase your product at a local landmark. A newsletter might highlight customer stories or upcoming community events.

How about making a local resource guide? This could be a list of emergency numbers, a calendar of community events, or favorite local recipes. It should be something practical that folks would want to keep and refer to – and with your business name on it, they'll remember who gave it to them.

Finally, let's measure how well your content is doing. Are people commenting, sharing, or coming into your store and mentioning it? Those are good signs. But also, ask for feedback. When customers come in, ask them if they saw your latest post or guide and what they thought. Their answers will help you make even better content next time.

By following these guidelines, you'll create content that resonates with your local audience. It'll show them that you're not just a business owner; you're a neighbor who cares. And that's the kind of connection that can turn a local into a loyal customer.

So go on, give it a try. Get to know your local crowd, talk about what matters to them, and create content that feels as familiar and comfortable as your favorite spot on the couch. That's how you'll win the hearts – and business – of your community.

Distributing Your Content Effectively

When you create something, you want people to see it, right? It's like making a big, beautiful cake. You wouldn't just leave it in the kitchen. You'd take it out where everyone can see it, smell it, and say, "Wow, that looks amazing!" The same goes for the content about your local business. You've made it. It's good. Now, how do we get it out there where the locals can enjoy it?

First, think about where people around you go to get information. Not all towns are the same. Some people love reading the newspaper at the diner. Others check their Facebook on the phone while waiting for the bus. Your job is to find out where your neighbors are looking and make sure your content shows up there.

Let's say you run a bakery in town. You've written a great post about the secret behind your famous carrot cake. Who wouldn't want to read that? But where do you put it? You could put it on a blog on your website. That's one good place. But is that where your local customers are going to see it? Maybe not. So, what else can you do?

Well, you can share that post on social media. You can use Facebook because lots of people check their Facebook feeds. You might also use Instagram and take a really nice picture of the cake to go with the post. People love seeing tasty food pictures. They might even share it with their friends!

Now, don't forget about email. You can send the post out in a newsletter. If people signed up to hear from you, they're saying, "Hey, I like this place. Tell me more." So, give them what they want. They'll be happy to get a fun email from you, and they might come in to try that cake.

But how about people who don't go online much? You've still got options. You could print a little flyer with the secret recipe and a picture. Then, hand it out to customers in your bakery or leave some at the counter. People like free stuff, especially recipes. And they might pass it to a friend or pin it on their fridge. That's more eyes on your content.

Another smart move is to join local events. Is there a town fair coming up? Maybe a farmers' market? You can set up a booth and hand out samples of that famous carrot cake along with your recipe flyers. Talk to people. Tell them about your post. Maybe even show it on a tablet. People get excited when they meet the person behind a business. It makes them feel a special connection.

What about local influencers? These are people in your town who lots of folks listen to. They might be on the radio or have a popular blog. Make friends with them. Share your content with them. If they like it, they might talk about it. And if they talk about it, more people will hear about your bakery. It's like getting a thumbs up from someone everyone respects.

Don't forget to ask your customers to help you. When they come into your shop, ask if they saw your post. If they did and they liked it, ask them to tell their friends or share it online. People often want to help, especially if they like your business and what you do.

There's also a little thing called ads. You can run ads in the local paper or online. It costs money, but it's a way to make sure even more people see your content. Just be clear about what you want. Do you want them to read your post? Visit your shop? Try that carrot cake? Make sure your ad says exactly what you're hoping people will do.

Lastly, keep track of what works. Did a lot of people come in after you handed out flyers at the fair? Did someone say they saw your post on Facebook? Write it down. It's important to know what's working. That way, you can do more of what brings people to your bakery and less of what doesn't. It's like making sure you put the right amount of sugar in your cake. Too little and it's not sweet enough. Too much and it's too sweet. You want to get it just right.

So, you see? Distributing your content is about thinking where your customers are and meeting them there. It's about being friendly and asking for help when you need it. And it's about keeping your eyes open to see what brings people through your door. That's how you make sure your content isn't just sitting around. It's out there, doing its job, bringing local folks into your shop, and making them happy. And happy customers often come back for more.

Remember, this isn't just about selling carrot cake. It's about creating a community around your bakery, where people know you and you know them. It's about sharing what you love and what you're good at. Keep it simple, be consistent, and be where your customers are. That's how you distribute your content effectively and make your local business a place people love to talk about and visit.

Measuring Content Success

When we put our heart and soul into creating content, we want to know if it's working. It's not just about feeling good because we made something. We need to be sure it's helping our business. To do this, we look at special signs that tell us if our content is a hit or a miss. These signs are called Key Performance Indicators, or KPIs for short.

Think of KPIs like a game of soccer. When you're in the game, you keep track of goals to know who's winning. In the same way, KPIs are the goals we keep track of in our content game. They show us how well we are doing. Are people looking at our content? Do they like it? Do they do what we ask them to after reading it? These are the kinds of questions KPIs help us answer.

First off, we need to know if people are actually seeing our content. This is called reach. Just like when you shout in a large room, you want to know if people at the back can hear you. Reach tells us how far our content is going. Are enough people seeing it? Is our content reaching the back of the room?

Next, we look at how people behave with our content. Do they stay and read it all, or do they leave fast? This is called engagement. Imagine you're telling a story. You want to see that people are listening, not looking at their phones or walking away. If they listen to the whole story and ask questions, you know they are engaged. It's the same with content. If they read, click, comment, or share, they're into it, and that's good.

Another important sign is how often people do what we ask them to after seeing our content. This could be buying something, signing up for a newsletter, or visiting a store. We call this conversion. Think of it like inviting friends over. If you send out ten invites and eight friends show up, that's a good conversion. A lot of them did what you asked. If only two come, you'd wonder what went wrong.

But how do we keep track of all these signs? We use special tools made just for this job. These tools look at all the data and tell us about our reach, engagement, conversion, and more. Some tools are easy to use and even free. Others are more complex and cost money. The key is to pick the tools that are right for your business and the goals you have.

One popular tool is Google Analytics. It's like a detective that watches how people act on your website. It tells you how many came, how long they stayed, and what they looked at. It's a really useful tool to see if your content is working.

Another tool is social media analytics. These are built into platforms like Facebook, Instagram, and Twitter. They tell you all about how people interact with your content on these sites. How many saw it? How many liked it or shared it? This helps us see if our content is a hit on social media.

But remember, all these numbers and tools are to help us make decisions. They aren't just numbers for numbers' sake. They're like clues in a mystery that help us solve the case. If something's not working, we look at our KPIs to find out why and fix it.

One last thing. Don't get lost in the numbers. It's easy to do. Keep your eyes on what matters most. That's your business goals. Your content should always be helping you get closer to these goals. If it's not, even if the numbers look good, it's time to make a change.

To wrap it up, we use signs, or KPIs, to see if our content is doing its job. Tools help us do this. They're like helpers that give us the info we need. And we always match what we find with our business goals. That's how we know for sure that our content is a success.

So, when you make content next time, start by thinking of these KPIs. Set up the tools to track them. And keep your business goals in mind. Do this, and you'll be on your way to knowing if your content is really working for you. And that's a big win, for you and your business.

Recap: Content Marketing Mastery

Let's talk about what we've learned about content marketing. It is something that helps you connect with people who live near you, who might come to your store or use your service. This is about how to share what you do with them in a way that they will like and remember.

First, we learned why sharing information about what you do is so important. It helps people in your town or city know about your business. It can make them trust you more, too. When you tell them interesting things, they start to see you as someone who knows a lot. And that's good for your business.

Then, we talked about making a plan for what you want to tell people. You thought about what goals you have for your business. You used those goals to decide what kind of things you want to talk about. You made a calendar so you could keep sharing new things all the time without forgetting or getting too busy.

After that, we looked at what kind of things to talk about. You learned how to make sure what you say is something people nearby will care about. You thought about what they like and what they need. And you learned about different kinds of ways to share information, like stories, pictures, or helpful tips.

Next, you found out how to get your information out there. You picked the best places to share your stories so that many local people would see them. You also learned how to tell more people about what you have shared. This is so that you can reach more people who might walk into your store or ask for your service.

Then, we talked about how to know if what you are sharing is working. You learned about things to look at that show if people are interested in what you're telling them. You also learned about tools that can help you see how well your stories are doing.

Let's say you own a coffee shop. You have followed all these steps. You have shared stories about where your coffee comes from and how you make it. You have posted pictures of customers enjoying your coffee. You have given tips on how to make great coffee at home. You have put this on social media where a lot of people in your city see it. You have also checked to see that people are liking and talking about what you shared.

Now, here's a checklist to help you keep doing this well:

- Make sure you always know what your goals are for your business.
- Plan what you want to say about your business. Write it on a calendar.
- Think about what local people like and need when you decide what to talk about.
- Pick the best places to share your stories so a lot of local people will see them.
- Find ways to tell even more people about your stories, like asking

friends to share them or putting them in a local newspaper.

- Keep an eye on how many people like, share, and talk about your stories. Use tools that help you see this easily.

By following these steps, you are taking big steps towards making your business more known and liked in your area. People will start to see you as someone who gives them good information and who cares about the same things they do. And when they think about the service you offer, they will think of you first.

Remember, it's all about being helpful and interesting. Keep sharing things that help people and make them smile or think. If you do this, they will come to your store or use your service, and they will tell their friends about you, too. This is how you use content marketing to make your business grow and become an important part of your community.

Advanced Local SEO Techniques

Exploring Hyperlocal SEO

Hyperlocal SEO is like a magnifying glass for your business on the internet. It's about shining a bright light on your shop, café, or office, in the neighborhood where you are. This is important because people close by are often the ones who will walk through your door and become customers. They might be just around the corner, looking for exactly what you offer. But if they can't find you online, they'll never know you're there.

So let's dive into hyperlocal SEO. It's a more focused type of local SEO. Instead of covering a whole city, it zeroes in on small areas. Think of neighborhoods, streets, or even buildings. It's for businesses that know their neighbors are their best bet for customers. It could be a bakery, a hair salon, or a bookstore. These places want folks nearby to find them first, not someone from far away.

Good hyperlocal SEO makes sure that when someone nearby searches for what you sell or do, your business pops up on their screen. It's like putting up the biggest sign in your neighborhood, but on the internet. This matters because more and more people search for things "near me" on their phones. When they do, you want to be the answer they get.

Now, how do you make sure your business is the one they find? You start with your website. Make sure it says exactly where you are. Not just the city, but the neighborhood or street. If you're in a big building, say which part. It's like telling a friend how to find your house, using landmarks they know.

Next, you get your business on local listings. Websites like Google My Business, Yelp, and others help people find what they need in their area. It's like putting your name in the local phone book, but online. When you're on these sites, make sure all your details are right. The address, phone number, and what you do should all be clear and the same everywhere.

Reviews are also a big part of hyperlocal SEO. When people say nice things about your business online, it's like they're telling their friends about you. And just like in real life, their friends are more likely to come and see what the fuss is about. So encourage your happy customers to leave reviews on local listing sites. It can make a big difference.

But it's not just about being listed and getting reviews. You also need to talk about your area on your website and in your posts. Mention local events, streets, and landmarks. It's like joining in on the neighborhood chat. It shows you're part of the community and helps people and search engines see you're really there.

And remember, all this has to be easy to read on a phone. Most people use their phones to search for things nearby. If your website is hard to read on a small screen, they might give up and go somewhere else. Keep it simple and clear.

So, that's the what and the why of hyperlocal SEO. It's about being found by the people who are most likely to walk in your door. You make sure your business shows up where and when they're looking. You're right there in their pocket, on their phone, just when they need you.

Now let's talk about how you can use hyperlocal SEO to shine online. You can start by checking your website. Is it clear where you're located? Can people find your address and phone number in seconds? If not, fix that first. Then, go and claim your spot on local listing sites. Make sure they all match and are up-to-date.

Ask your customers to share their love for your business online. Each review is a little beacon, drawing more people to you. Get involved in local events and use them in your marketing. Talk about your neighborhood and its landmarks. Show pictures of your place, especially if it's got something special about it.

But the best part? This isn't just good for your customers. It's good for you too. When your business is easy to find and well-liked locally, you become the go-to spot. You're the first name that comes to mind when someone needs what you offer. That's the power of hyperlocal SEO. It brings your neighbors to you, one click at a time.

So there you have it. You now know what hyperlocal SEO is and why it's like a neighborhood party and you're the guest of honor. You've got the steps to take to make sure your business is the one people find and choose. It's time to get out there and be the local star. Your neighborhood is waiting for you. All you need to do is show up in their searches.

Schema Markup for Local Businesses

So, you have a local business. You want people to find you when they type things into search engines. Not just any people, but the ones right in your area who are looking for what you offer. There's a secret ingredient to help you stand out. It's called schema markup. This might sound fancy, but it's just a special code that makes search engines understand your website better. Let's dig into it.

Think of schema markup as a highlighter. When you read a book, you might use a highlighter to mark the important stuff. Schema markup does the same for your website. It tells search engines, like Google, exactly what's important about your business. It could be your address, the services you offer, or your opening hours.

Why is this important, you ask? Well, because when people search for things, search engines want to give them the best answers. Schema markup makes it easier for search engines to pick your business as a good answer. It can help your local business show up better in search results. This means more people clicking on your site, which can lead to more customers.

Now, let's get your hands dirty and walk through putting schema markup to work for you. First, you'll want to go to a website that makes this code. There are free tools out there. Google's Structured Data Markup Helper is one you can use. You pick what kind of local business you are and then start filling in the blanks. You'll tell it about your business name, address, phone number, and more.

After you fill in your details, this tool will spit out some code. This is your schema markup. The next step is to put this code on your website. You'll need to add it to the right spot in your website's code. If you're not sure how to do this, it's okay to ask for some help. You can ask a friend who knows about websites or hire someone to do it.

Once you've added the schema markup to your site, you're not done yet. You need to check if it's working right. Google has another tool for this, the Structured Data Testing Tool. You put in your website's address, and it tells you if you did everything right or if there's something you need to fix. If there's a mistake, it'll show you where it is.

Putting schema markup on your site is something you have to do carefully. But when you do it right, it's like giving search engines a map to your business. And that map leads more customers right to your door. Just remember, this isn't a one-time job. You need to keep your schema markup up to date. If you change your phone number or move to a new place, you need to update your schema markup too. Keep it fresh, keep it accurate, and it'll serve you well.

Now, you may be wondering, does this really make a difference? The answer is yes. Search engines are getting smarter, but they still need our help to understand exactly what our websites are about. By using schema markup, you're doing just that. You're making it crystal clear what you offer and where you are. This is a big deal in the crowded online world. In that crowd, anything that helps you stand out is a tool you want to use.

So, that's the scoop on schema markup. It's a powerful tool for your local business. It takes a bit of effort to set up, but the rewards are worth it. Better visibility in search results means more eyes on your business. And more eyes can mean more customers walking through your door. It's a step that can bring real value to your local search efforts. Now, take this knowledge and make it work for you. Get that schema markup on your site and watch how it can help your local business shine online.

Mobile Optimization for Local Search

There is something everyone with a business needs to know. These days, when people want something, they grab their phones. They look for places to eat, shops to buy from, and services to help them. That's why your website needs to work well on phones. It's not just good to have; it's a must-have. Now, let's talk about what makes a website great for phone users and why it matters.

First things first. Your website has to be easy to use on a phone. This means it should look good and be easy to read. No one likes to pinch and zoom just to read a menu or find your phone number. If they do, they might just give up and go somewhere else. So, your website has to change shape to fit whatever screen it's on. This is called responsive design. It's like a magic trick for websites. It makes sure your website can fit on any screen, big or small, like a puzzle piece that fits everywhere.

Now, here's the deal. When people use their phones to look for something, they want it fast. If your website takes longer than a few seconds to load, people may leave. That's why your website's speed is key. It's like being in a race where every second counts. You want to be the fastest, so people stay and see what you have to offer. To do this, you have to make sure pictures and videos on your site are not too big because they can slow things down.

Another part of making your site great for phones is the way it feels. When someone taps a button, it should work the first time. They should be able to find what they need without getting lost. The menu should be simple, and contact information should be easy to find. Think of it like this: Your website is like a guide in a big city. It should help people find their way around easily and quickly. If it's good, they will want to come back again or tell their friends about it.

So far, we've talked about how your website should fit on all screens, be super fast, and easy to use. Now, let's get into some steps you can take to make this happen. It's important because these steps will help more people find your business when they search on their phones.

The first step is to check how your site looks on different devices. There are tools on the internet that let you do this. Use them to see how your website looks on phones and tablets. This helps you understand what others see when they visit your site on their phones. If something looks off, you know you need to fix it.

Next up is testing your site's speed. There are free tools for this too. They tell you how fast your site loads and what you can do to make it faster. It might say your pictures are too big or you have too much stuff on your page. Listen to what it says and make those changes. It's like tuning up a car to make it run better.

Now, let's talk about the buttons and links on your site. Make them big enough to tap with a finger. If they're too small, it's hard to click them without making a mistake. You don't want people getting frustrated because they can't press the right button. And make sure your site is neat. Keep the important stuff like your phone number, address, and hours right at the top or in an easy spot to find. That way, people can find what they need and contact you without any trouble.

Last but not least, keep your content up to date. Make sure your business hours, services, and prices are current. When people look for a business, they trust the information they find online. If it's wrong, they might feel let down. You don't want that. Keep everything fresh and true, so people know they can rely on what they see.

So there you have it. A friendly guide to making your website awesome for local search on phones. It's all about being fast, fitting on all screens, and easy to use. If you do these things, you'll help people find and like your business. And that's what you want, right? To be the place people turn to when they need something you offer. So take these steps, make your website shine on phones, and watch as more people come your way.

Local SEO for Voice Search

Have you ever asked your phone for the nearest coffee shop? That's voice search. It's like talking to a friend who knows all the places around. And it's getting big. Really big. So, we need to get your local business ready for it. People are talking to their phones more. They ask for places to eat, shop, and find fun things to do. And we want them to find you.

First things first, voice search is different from typing. When we talk, we use long sentences. We ask full questions. We say things like, "Where's the closest pet store that sells tropical fish?" But when we type, we might just put "pet store near me." See the difference? One is like a chat and the other is just a few words.

Now, let's make sure that when someone asks their phone for something you offer, they find you. It's about being smart with words. We call these words 'keywords'. For voice search, we use long keywords. They are like little trails that lead people to your business. We call them 'long-tail keywords'. They're not just one word; they're a bunch of words, like a sentence.

To find these keywords, think like a customer. What would you ask for if you were looking for your business? Write those sentences down. Those are your long-tail keywords. Put them on your website. But it's not just about putting them anywhere. They have to fit in, sound natural. Like how you would tell a friend about what you offer.

Then, there's the 'Google My Business' page. It's a place where you tell Google about your business. You say where you are, when you're open, and what you do. Make sure all the info there is right. If it's wrong, people might not find you. Or worse, they might show up when you're closed. That's not good.

Also, answer questions people might ask. Like, "What time do you close?" or "Do you have Wi-Fi?" Put those answers on your website and your Google My Business page. Be clear and simple. That helps voice search find you.

Something else that's cool is 'featured snippets'. That's a box that shows up on Google when it really likes an answer. You want to get in that box. So, answer questions really well. Write like you speak. Be helpful. Google might put you in that box so people see you first.

Now, here's something important. Your website has to load fast. Think about it. When you ask a friend something, you want the answer quick, right? It's the same with voice search. Make sure your website is speedy. That way, when someone asks for something you offer, they get the answer fast.

And remember, people use voice search everywhere. They might be walking or even driving. So, your website needs to work well on phones and tablets. Make sure it looks good and is easy to use on all devices.

Finally, keep your business info everywhere the same. If your hours are 9 to 5, say 9 to 5 everywhere. On your website, on your Google My Business, on social media. Everywhere. That way, no matter how someone asks for you, they get the right info.

So, let's wrap it up. Voice search is talking to find stuff. Use long sentences as keywords. Put them on your site so they sound like you're having a chat. Check your Google My Business page is right. Answer questions clearly. Try to get into the featured snippets. Make sure your site is fast and works on phones. Keep your info the same everywhere. Do these things, and when someone asks their phone for what you offer, they'll find you. That's great for business, right?

Give these steps a try. Take it slow. Make sure you do it right. And watch as more people find and choose your business just by asking their phone a question. It's pretty cool when you think about it. And you can do it. Start today and get ready for the future of search.

Leveraging Local Partnerships and Events

When we think about local SEO, we often consider the technical bits. Things like keywords, business listings, and online reviews. Yet, there's a whole world out there, right in your local area, full of opportunities to boost your SEO in a way that feels close to home. We're talking about actual places, events, and other local businesses that you can connect with.

Let's dive into this. Think about your local area. It's full of businesses, right? When you form partnerships with these businesses, you create a network. A helpful network that can support your business – and you can support theirs. It's like having friends who help each other out. But how does this help your SEO? Well, it can help a lot, and I'll tell you why and how.

Firstly, when you team up with another local business, you can share each other's links on your websites. This is called link building. It's like telling search engines, "Hey, we trust each other, and we're connected." Search engines see this and think your site must be helpful and trustworthy. That could help your website show up better in search results.

Now, about events. Local events are a goldmine for SEO. When you get involved in events, you get to talk about them on your website. You can write about the event beforehand, during, and even after it's all done. You can post pictures, talk about what you learned, and share stories from the event. Every bit of this is content that search engines love. Why? Because it's fresh, it's local, and it's relevant.

Here's how you can do this. Let's say there's a local fair coming up. You decide to join in. Maybe you set up a booth, or you sponsor part of the fair. You can then write a blog post to tell your customers all about it. In that post, you can include the event's name, where it's at, when it's happening, and what you'll be doing there. This is the kind of information people search for. And if your post can answer their questions, search engines take notice.

Now, after the event is over, you're not done yet. You can write a follow-up post. Share what went well, who you met, and what you learned. You can even ask people who visited your booth to leave a comment on your post or share their own photos with you. When people interact with your content like this, it shows search engines that your site is a lively place where people want to be.

But how do you make sure you're doing this right? Let's get into that. For link building with local businesses, you want to make sure you're picking the right partners. Look for businesses that are related to yours in some way. Maybe they're not exactly the same as your business, but they should be close enough that it makes sense for you to be linked together.

For example, if you run a bakery, you might partner with the local coffee shop. You could agree to link to each other's websites. You might write a blog post about the best breakfast spots in town and mention them. They might do the same and talk about where to find the best pastries. This way, you're helping each other out in a way that feels natural and makes sense to people - and to search engines.

With events, you want to be a bit more strategic. You should pick events that your customers would be interested in. If you sell sports equipment, a local marathon might be a great event to get involved in. You can write about training tips, what gear to use, and even offer a special discount for participants. This attracts the right kind of attention from the right kind of people – those who are interested in what you have to offer.

The key to all of this is to stay genuine. You're not just doing this for SEO. You're doing it to connect with your community and be a part of it. That genuine connection is what really makes this strategy shine. And it's what will set you apart from the competition. Not everyone is willing to put in the effort to build these relationships and create this content. But you are. And that's what's going to make a difference.

So, let's recap what you can do right now. Look around your local area for businesses you can partner with. Reach out to them and suggest linking to each other's sites. And keep an eye out for local events that align with your business. Get involved and make sure to talk about it online, before, during, and after the event. This is how you can make local partnerships and events a powerful part of your local SEO strategy. It's simple, it's actionable, and it can make a real difference for your business.

Recap: Navigating Advanced Local SEO

So, we have journeyed through the world of advanced local SEO together. Think of SEO as a map. This map has many paths and we've explored some of the less traveled ones. The goal? To lead people straight to our doorstep. Now, let's take a deep breath and walk through what we've learned. It's about making sure you've got all the tools in your belt to stand out in your neighborhood on the internet.

First off, we talked about getting very specific with our SEO. Like, super specific. This means not just saying you're in a big city, but saying exactly where in that city you are. Maybe it's a side street next to that big doughnut shop everyone loves. That's hyperlocal SEO. It's like telling your friend exactly where to find you at a big party.

Then, we dove into something called schema markup. That's a fancy way of saying we make it extra clear to search engines what our business is all about. It's like when you speak very clearly so someone can understand you better. This way, when someone asks Google about a local business, yours pops up nice and clear.

Remember how everyone is using their phones all the time? Well, we want to make sure they can find us easily on those little screens. We need to make sure our websites load fast and look good on phones. That's mobile optimization. It's like making sure your shop's sign is big and bright enough to be seen from across the street.

Oh, and let's not forget about voice search. These days, a lot of people just ask their phones for help instead of typing. We need to make our business sound good to those digital assistants. It's like making sure you sound friendly and helpful when someone calls your shop.

We also can't do everything alone, right? So we talked about making friends with other local businesses and being part of community events. That's like showing up to the neighborhood barbecue and making sure everyone knows who you are and what you do. It's good for the community and good for your business.

Now, let's make sure all this sticks. We're going to go over some steps you can take right away to make sure you're using all these fancy SEO techniques. This is your action plan. Follow these steps, and you'll be on your way to being a local SEO superstar.

- Look at your website and see if you've told the internet exactly where you are. Not just the city, but the spot on the map. If not, update it.
- Check if your website talks clearly to search engines. If you're not sure, ask someone who knows about schema markup. They can help make your site speak search engine language.
- Grab a phone and open up your website. Does it take a long time to load? Is it hard to read? If yes, it's time to make your site better for mobile.
- Practice talking to your phone. Ask it questions people might ask about your business. See what it says back. If your business isn't coming up, look into voice search SEO.
- Reach out to other businesses near you. See if you can help each other out. Maybe you can share posts about each other on social media.
- Look for events in your area. Can you join in? Can you sponsor them? Get involved. It's a great way to spread the word about your business.
  By ticking each of these off your list, you're not just doing SEO.

You're building connections. You're making sure when someone in your town needs what you offer, they find you first. You're helping your community and helping your business. It's a win-win.

So, there you have it. A recap and an action plan for advanced local SEO. Keep this in mind: the world of search engines changes all the time. We must keep learning and adjusting. But if you follow these steps, you'll be heading in the right direction.

And remember, taking action is key. Reading about these tips is good, but doing them is what makes the difference. So, let's not just sit on this knowledge. Let's use it. Let's make our businesses shine in the local search world.

The Role of Call Tracking in Local Marketing

Overview of Call Tracking

What is call tracking? It's a way to know where your phone calls come from. Think about it. You run a local business, and you put your phone number everywhere. On your website, flyers, and ads. But how do you know which one works best? That's where call tracking helps. It gives each spot a different phone number. Then, when someone calls, you know exactly where they saw your number. Smart, right?

People still use phones a lot. Even though we text and email, a good old phone call is personal. It's real. That's why for local businesses, calls are gold. Each call could be a new customer. Or an old one coming back. So we need to treat calls like treasure. And to find treasure, we need the right map. Call tracking is that map.

Why is this map so special? Well, it tells you more than just where calls come from. It tells you what people care about. Maybe they saw an ad about a sale and called. That means the sale is working. Or maybe they found you online and called after reading reviews. That shows your online presence is strong. This kind of info is more than just useful. It's powerful. It helps you make good choices for your business.

Importance for ROI

Now, let's talk about money. We all care about it, especially in business. ROI stands for return on investment. It answers a big question: "Am I making more money than I'm spending on my ads?" Call tracking can help answer that.

Without call tracking, you might be throwing money away. You spend on ads, but which ones bring you customers? It's like having a bunch of buckets to catch rain. But if you don't check them, you won't know which one is full. You might miss out on the best water. With call tracking, you can check those buckets. You see which ads fill them up with calls. Then, you can spend your money where it works best.

Imagine you put an ad in the local paper. And you put one on a website. You get calls, but where do they come from? With call tracking, you know. Say the paper ad brings two calls, but the website brings twenty. Now you know. The website is where you should put more of your money. That's smart business. That's good ROI.

So, why do we care about ROI? It's simple. You want your business to grow. To make more money. To serve more people. And to do that, you need to know what works. Call tracking shows you that. It's like having a helper who whispers in your ear, "This is working. Do more of this." And that's something every business owner needs.

Some people might think this sounds hard. But it isn't. It's just about getting the right tools and using them well. And that's what we're here for. To make sure you have those tools. And to make sure you know how to use them. That's how you make your business better. That's how you serve your community better. And isn't that what it's all about?

So, let's keep it simple. Call tracking helps you see what's working. It helps you spend your money wisely. And it helps you grow your business. It's a simple idea. But it's one that can change everything. And that's why it's so important.

There you have it. Call tracking is a key part of local marketing. It helps you understand your customers better. It shows you where to spend your money. And it helps you make smart choices for your business. It's not just about tracking calls. It's about making each call count. It's about growing your business and serving your community. And that's what we're all here to do.

Setting Up Call Tracking Systems

If you run a service-based business, knowing who calls you and why is like finding a treasure map. It shows you where your customers come from and how they find you. This is where setting up a call tracking system comes into play. It's something that can truly change the game for you. So, let's walk through how to get this up and running, shall we?

First things first, you need to pick a call tracking provider. But hold on, don't just go for the first one you see. This choice is a big deal. It's like choosing a new friend. You want someone reliable, right? So, you look for a provider that's easy to use, fits your budget, and gives you all the details on your calls. They should tell you where your calls come from, which ads they are responding to, and even record the calls if you need that.

Now, when you find a few options, check how they work. It should be a piece of cake to set up. Look for something that doesn't make you scratch your head with lots of tech talk. And, they should be friendly, always there to help you when you get stuck.

Once you've picked your call tracking buddy, it's time to set it up. Here's what you do. You'll get a bunch of phone numbers from your provider.

Think of these like new doors for customers to walk through to reach you. You put these numbers in your ads, on your website, and anywhere else you talk to people. Then, when someone rings you up, the call tracking system takes notes. It notes where they're calling from, which door they walked through, and it can even record what you both say on the call.

Doing this is super helpful because later, you can listen and learn from these calls. You can hear what your customers like and what they don't. You can even find out if they're saying something special that makes them decide to use your service. This is pure gold for your business.

But wait, there's more. You don't just set this up and forget it. Nope. You keep an eye on it, like a gardener watches their plants. You see which phone numbers bring in the most calls. If one number is getting lots of rings, that's a sign that the ad or the web page it's on is working big time.

And if some numbers are quiet, like a library, then you know something's not right. Maybe the ad is in the wrong place, or it's not catchy enough. This is your chance to change things and make them better. Try a new ad or a new spot for it and see if more calls come in. It's all about testing and improving, just like a chef tries different spices to make their food taste amazing.

What else? Ah, yes. Make sure your team knows about this. If you have people answering the calls, train them. Tell them how important every call is. It's not just a ring; it's someone who might need your help. Every call is a chance to show how great you are and to make a new friend or customer.

And remember, this isn't just about getting more calls. It's about making each call count. Use what you learn from the tracking system to make every call a chance to grow your business. Make each word you say, and every answer you give, something that makes the person on the other end smile and think, "Yes, this is the right choice."

In the end, setting up a call tracking system is one of the best moves you can make. It gives you a map to understand your customers, how to reach more people like them, and how to keep them happy. And when customers are happy, they come back. They tell their friends about you. Your business grows. So, take the time to set this up right, keep an eye on it, and use what you learn to make your service the best it can be. It's an action you can take today that can really make a difference for tomorrow.

Analyzing Call Data for Marketing Insights

When you have call tracking set up for your business, you start to gather lots of information. This information, or call data, is like a treasure map. It can lead you to understand your customers better. So let's talk about what this data is and why it's so valuable.

Call data includes the time of the call, how long it lasted, and where it came from. It tells you which ads or web pages made someone pick up the phone. This might seem simple, but it's very powerful. You get to see what is working in your marketing.

Now, you might ask, "Why is this important?" Well, knowing what makes your phone ring helps you make smart choices. It means you can spend money on ads that work and stop using ones that don't. It's like choosing to put your money in a winning team.

Here's how to start with analyzing call data. First, look at the times you get the most calls. Are there more calls in the morning or afternoon? This helps you know when to have more staff ready to answer calls. It's important because you want to talk to as many customers as you can. If you miss their calls, they might go to someone else.

Next, check which ads or web pages bring in the most calls. If you see one ad brings in a lot of calls, that's great! It means that ad speaks to people. You might want to use the same words or pictures in other ads too.

Understanding the length of calls can also give you clues. If calls are short, people might not be getting the help they need. If they are long, maybe your team is doing a great job explaining your services. Or, it might mean they are spending too much time on things that are not so important. You need to find a good balance.

Another thing to think about is where the calls are coming from. If you notice that calls come from a certain place, that's where your customers are. You might want to do more marketing in that area. It's like seeing where the fish are biting and then fishing more in that spot.

Now, let's talk about making decisions with your call data. We know it's important to use our data to make smart moves. For example, if you see a certain ad makes your phone ring a lot, you might want to put more money into that ad. It's working, so let's do more of it.

But it's not just about spending more money. It's also about making your ads better. You can look at the words in the ads that work well. Use those words in other ads too. It's like if you find a good recipe, you use the same ingredients to make other dishes tasty too.

There's something else that's very cool about call data. It can tell you about your team. If you see that one person is very good at turning callers into customers, they are doing something right. You can learn from them. Have them share their tips with the rest of the team. It's like when someone is good at a game, you watch and learn how to be good too.

Remember, the most important part of all this is action. You have to use your call data to make changes. It's not enough to just look at the information. You have to act on it. It's like knowing you have a map to treasure but never going to look for it. You need to follow the map and find the treasure.

So, take your call data and think about it. What does it tell you about your customers? What does it say about your marketing? What can you learn from your team? Use all this information to make your business better. It's a powerful tool that can help you grow and serve your customers better.

In the end, call data is a big help in making your business shine. It's all about listening to what the data is telling you and taking action. This way, your business can keep getting better every day. And that means happy customers and a happy you.

Optimizing for Phone Call Conversions

When you have a business, one key to success is making sure that when people call you, they end up happy and ready to use your service. Think about it like making a great recipe. You want to mix the right ingredients so that your customers enjoy what you give them and want to come back for more. This is what we call optimizing for phone call conversions. It's a way of making sure that when people ring you up, more of those calls turn into sales or appointments. Now, let's take a gentle walk through the steps you need to take to make this happen, shall we?

First things first, you've got to look at your current phone calls. If you have a team that answers the phone, it's like having a group of chefs in a kitchen. You need to make sure they have the best recipes and ingredients – in this case, the right words and a friendly voice. To do this, you must listen to how they talk to customers and then think about ways to make it even better.

One way to improve is to have a clear guide for your team. This means writing down the most important things they should say and do on a call. For example, they should always say hello with a smile in their voice. They should ask the caller's name and use it during the conversation. It's like when you go to your favorite shop, and the person there knows your name – it feels good and makes you want to go back.

But there's more to it than just being nice. Your team also needs to know all about what you're selling. They need to answer questions, give details, and help the caller understand why your service is the best choice for them. It's like if someone asks you why your homemade cookies are so tasty, you'd tell them about the special chocolate you use or how you bake them with care.

Training your staff is super important. They need to practice the guide you've written for them until it feels easy and natural. It's like learning to ride a bike. At first, it's hard, and you might wobble, but with practice, it becomes a breeze. Your team needs to know the guide so well that they can still sound friendly and not like robots. They need to be ready for any kind of question or worry that a caller might have.

Let's talk about practice. Just like a basketball player shoots hoops over and over, your team should practice calls a lot. Role-playing can help here. That means one person pretends to be the customer, and another is the staff member. They try out different situations to see what works best. It's fun, and it helps your team get ready for the real thing.

Remember, every call is a chance to make a sale. So, you want to make sure your team knows how to lead the conversation to that point. They need to be gentle but also clear about what steps the caller should take next. Maybe it's setting up an appointment or saying yes to a service. It's like guiding someone down a path to a lovely picnic spot. You make sure they don't get lost and that they're happy when they get there.

After the call, there's one more step. Your team should write down what happened. They need to keep track of what the caller wanted, any questions they had, and what the result was. This is important because it helps you see patterns. Maybe lots of people are asking about something you don't offer yet. That could be a hint that you should add it to your services. It's like noticing that people keep asking for chocolate chip ice cream – if you only have vanilla, maybe it's time to start making chocolate chip, too.

Finally, keep checking on how things are going. Every once in a while, listen to calls and read the notes your team has made. See if there's anything you can improve. It's like tweaking a recipe until it's just right. Maybe you need to change some words in your guide or give your team more information on a new service. It's all about making it better and better, so more callers turn into happy customers.

So there you have it. By taking good care of your phone calls, you can help your business grow. It's about having a friendly, knowledgeable team, a clear guide for them to follow, lots of practice, and always looking for ways to do even better. Do these things, and you'll be on your way to making every call count.

Remember, every step you take to improve phone call conversions is like planting seeds in a garden. With care, those seeds will grow into strong plants. In the same way, by focusing on making great phone calls, you will see your business flourish. Take these tips, use them every day, and watch your business thrive!

Integrating Call Tracking with Other Marketing Tools

Now, let's chat about putting call tracking together with other marketing tools you have. It's like putting together pieces of a puzzle. Each piece is good on its own. But when you put them all together? That's when you see the whole picture.

First things first, we set up call tracking. It's a bit like a diary for your business calls. Every call tells a story. Who called, why they called, and what they wanted. Now, picture that diary linking arms with all the other diaries from your business. Your sales records, your emails, your ads. They're all friends now, sharing what they know. That's integration.

Why do we care about this? Simple. When we know where things come from, we can make them better. If you run an ad and folks start calling, you want to know that ad is working. The call tracking is your proof. So, you pat that ad on the back and say, "Good job!" Then, you go make more ads like that one.

But how do we do this? First, we pick tools that like to talk to each other. Some tools are friendly. They have built-in ways to share info. Others? Not so much. You might need a bit of tech help to get them chatting. It's okay to ask for help; that's what smart people do.

Once they're talking, you watch. You see which ads bring you calls. What times people like to call. You might learn that folks call after seeing your Facebook post at lunchtime. Good to know, right? That means lunchtime is a great time to post.

And there's more. Maybe you send emails. Someone reads your email, likes it, and calls you. Your call tracking tells you, "Hey, that call came from the email!" Now you're thinking, "I'll send more emails like that."

It's not just about knowing what works, though. It's about making everything better. Say you have an online shop. Someone clicks on your ad, looks around but doesn't buy anything. Later, they call you. They have questions. You answer, they're happy, and they buy something. Without call tracking, you might never know the ad helped. With it, you know the ad did something good, even if it wasn't a direct sale.

What else can you do? You can look at your calls and see if people ask the same questions. If they do, maybe your website needs clearer info. You make changes. Next thing you know, people call less with questions and more to buy.

But here's the real magic. When you make things better based on what you learn, people are happier. Happy people tell friends. Friends become new customers. It's a beautiful cycle, and it all starts with putting your tools together.

So, take your call tracking, your ads, your emails, and your sales. Bring them together. Watch what they teach you. Then use that knowledge to grow. It's like having a map to treasure. The treasure is more customers, and the map is your integrated tools. It's a map anyone can follow if they take the time to read it right.

Remember, even small changes can lead to big wins. And that's what we're here for. Big wins for your business, one call at a time.

So go ahead. Start linking those tools. Ask for help if you need it. Keep an eye on what's working. Make it better. And always, always use what you learn to help your customers. That's how you win in business. Not just for today, but for all the tomorrows to come.

Recap: Optimizing Client Acquisition Through Calls

Let's talk about what we've learned. We've covered a lot in this chapter about call tracking. Our main goal here is to get more clients. And we've seen how call tracking can help us. It's like having a super tool that tells us what's working and what's not. So, let's sum up what we've discovered together.

First, we learned that call tracking is a big deal for local marketing. It's all about knowing who calls your business and why. This helps you see if your ads are working. If people see your ad and then call you, it means your ad is doing its job. But if they don't, you might need to fix something. That's why call tracking is so useful.

We also talked about how call tracking can show us the money we make from our ads. This is called return on investment, or ROI. It's a way of seeing if the money we spend on ads is worth it. If we spend $100 on ads and get $300 back in sales, that's a good ROI. Call tracking helps us see that clearly.

Next, we went through how to set up call tracking. This part is all about picking the right call tracking service and putting it into action. We looked at what makes a good call tracking service and how to get it running in your business. This step is like laying down the foundation for a house. It's got to be done right, or nothing else will work.

After that, we dove into understanding call data. We saw the kinds of information we can get from call tracking. Each call tells a story. It tells us what the caller wants, and sometimes how they found us. Knowing this can help us make smart choices about our marketing. It's like being a detective, finding clues that lead us to make our business better.

We also learned how to get more customers over the phone. This part is about making each call count. It's like when someone walks into a shop. You want to greet them and help them find what they need. On the phone, it's the same. We talked about training our team to be great at talking to callers. This can turn someone just asking about our service into a happy customer.

Then, we explored how call tracking works with other marketing tools. It's not just sitting by itself. It's part of a bigger picture. Call tracking data can be mixed with info from other marketing sources. This gives us a full view of how our business is doing. It's like putting together a puzzle. Each piece adds up to show us the whole image.

Now, here are some steps you can take right away to make call tracking work for you:

- **Choose a call tracking service:** Look at the options and pick one that fits your budget and needs.
- **Set it up:** Follow the steps to get call tracking running in your business. Ask for help if you need it.
- **Train your team:** Teach the people answering your phones how to turn callers into customers.
- **Check the data:** Regularly look at your call tracking reports to see what's working and what's not.
- **Take action:** Use what you learn from the data to make changes in your marketing. Try new things and see if they work better.
- **Keep learning:** Marketing changes all the time. Stay open to new ideas and keep improving your call tracking strategy.

By following these steps, you can start getting more out of your calls. This means more customers and more growth for your business. It's all about taking action. Knowing stuff is good, but doing stuff is what really counts.

So, let's wrap this up. You now have the know-how to make call tracking a powerful part of your business. It's time to put this knowledge into action and watch your business grow. You've got this!

Tracking Success and Measuring ROI

Defining Success in Local Marketing

Success in local marketing lights up like a bright sign for a business. It tells everyone, "We're here, and we're doing great!" To see that sign shine, you need to set goals. Goals are like a map. They show you where you want to go. And just like a map, they need to be clear. This way, you can follow them without getting lost.

But how do you set these goals? Start simple. Ask yourself what you want to see your business do. Do you want more people coming into your store? Maybe you want more people to call you. Or you want to sell more of something special you offer. Whatever it is, write it down. Make it as clear as daylight.

Once you know your goals, you need to figure out how to know if you're reaching them. This is where Key Performance Indicators (KPIs) come into play. KPIs are like signs along your path. They tell you if you're going the right way. Some KPIs might count how many people visit your website. Others might track how many of those visitors call your business. There are KPIs for almost everything you want to achieve.

But it's not just about numbers. It's about what those numbers mean for your business. You want to connect those KPIs to real things that happen. Like more sales, or having customers come back more often. This shows you if your local marketing is really working.

It's important to pick the right KPIs. If your goal is to get more people to visit your store, you might track how many people click on your online ads. If your goal is to sell more, you could look at how many people buy things from your website. Every goal needs its own special KPIs.

But remember, you have to be honest with yourself. If a KPI isn't showing good results, don't ignore it. That's like ignoring a sign that says "Wrong Way." Instead, use that sign to find a new way to your goal.

Let's talk about making these KPIs. First, sit down and think about what you really want for your business. Think hard. Be honest. Then, write it all down. Imagine it's a wish list for your business. These wishes are now your goals.

Next, look at your goals one by one. For each goal, think of a way to know if you're getting closer to it. This is your KPI. Write it down next to your goal. Now you have a map and signs to guide you. That's your plan for success in local marketing.

And when your plan is working, you'll see the changes. Maybe one day you look around and see more people in your store. Or your phone rings more. Or you get more emails asking about what you sell. That's when you know your local marketing is doing its job. And that's a great feeling.

To wrap it up, defining success in local marketing is all about knowing what you want and how to tell if you're getting it. It's about setting clear goals. It's about picking the right signs, or KPIs, to guide you. And it's about connecting those signs to real things that happen in your business. When you do all this, you're on your way to making your local marketing shine.

Now, with your goals and KPIs in hand, you're ready to step into the world of local marketing. You're ready to make your business stand out. And you're ready to see that bright sign of success light up for you.

Essential Tools for Tracking Local SEO Performance

Understanding how well your local SEO is doing is a lot like planting a garden. You put seeds in the ground. You water them. You make sure they get enough sun. Yet still, you need to keep checking to see how they are growing. You need tools for that. Good tools. Tools that tell you which plants are growing tall and which ones are not doing so well. When we talk about local SEO, these tools are like your gardening tools. They help you see what's working and what's not.

First, let's talk about what local SEO is. It's all about being easy to find when people near you are looking. Say you have a bakery. You want people in your town to find you when they search for "best birthday cake near me." Local SEO helps you be the answer they find. It's about being the top choice in your area.

Now, for the tools. There are lots of them out there. Some are simple. Some are more complex. But they all have the same goal: to give you clear information. What kind of information? Information like how many people visit your website. Where they come from. What words they used to find you. And if they took action like calling you or asking for directions.

One tool everybody hears about is Google Analytics. It's like a big report card for your website. It tells you how many visitors you have. It shows you graphs and numbers about their visits. It's very useful. And it's free to use. You just need a Google account to start.

To set up Google Analytics, you need to put a little piece of code on your website. This can sound scary, but it's not that hard. There are lots of guides that show you step by step how to do it. Once it's set up, Google starts collecting data. This data helps you see what's happening on your site.

But Google Analytics is not the only tool. Another good one is Google Search Console. This one helps you see how your website appears in Google search results. It can tell you if there are problems with your site that need fixing. Like if some pages are not showing up in search results. Or if there's something wrong that stops Google from understanding your site. Google Search Console is also free, which is nice.

Another tool worth talking about is called Ubersuggest. Ubersuggest helps you with keywords. Keywords are the words people type when searching for something. Ubersuggest tells you which keywords are popular. It also tells you how hard it might be to rank for those keywords. This means you can pick the best words to use to help people find you.

But remember, it's not just about finding any tool. It's about finding the right tools for you. Think about what you want to know. Do you want to see how many people call you from your website? You might want a tool like CallRail. CallRail tracks phone calls from your site. It tells you which ads or searches led to those calls. It can be very helpful to see what brings people to you.

Now, after choosing your tools, you have to use them. This part is like using a rain gauge in your garden. It's not enough to just have it. You need to read it and understand it. So, you need to check your tools often. Look at the numbers. See what they tell you. Learn from them.

Let's not forget about reviews. Reviews are very important for local businesses. There's a tool called Moz Local that can help you. Moz Local lets you manage your business listings across the web. It also helps you see and respond to reviews. This is important because good reviews can make more people want to visit you. And responding to reviews shows you care about your customers.

You don't have to be a computer genius to use these tools. Most of them are made to be user-friendly. They have help sections and customer support. They have videos that show you how to use them. You just need to take the time to learn.

And the best part? When you understand these tools, you can make better choices. You can see what parts of your local SEO are working best. You can see where you need to do more. Maybe you need better keywords. Or maybe you need to make your website easier for people to use on their phones. The tools help you understand. And when you understand, you can take action.

Remember, it's all about getting better. It's about seeing what you do well and doing more of that. And it's about seeing where you can improve and making changes. The tools don't do this for you. They give you the information you need to make these decisions yourself.

So think of your local SEO like a garden. Use your tools to check on it. Learn from what you see. Make changes where needed. And watch it grow. That's how you get better. That's how you help more people find you. And that's how you become the top choice in your area.

In the end, tracking your local SEO performance is not just about numbers. It's about understanding people. It's about connecting with them. It's about being the place they find when they need what you offer. And it's about making sure they have a good experience when they find you. This keeps them coming back. And it encourages them to tell others about you too.

So take your time. Choose your tools. Learn how to use them. Keep an eye on your data. And use what you learn to make your local SEO the best it can be. This is how you track success. This is how you grow your business.

And this is how you make sure you're always getting better at reaching the people around you.

Interpreting Data for Strategic Decisions

When we have lots of numbers and facts from our local marketing efforts, we need to know what they mean. It's like when we look up at the sky and see clouds. Just seeing them is not enough. We need to understand what the clouds are telling us about the weather. In the same way, we need to understand what our marketing numbers are telling us about our business.

Data analysis is a big word, but it's really just about asking the right questions. We look at the numbers to find answers. For example, we ask, "Did more people visit our website this month?" or "Did we sell more of our product after we posted that new ad online?" These questions help us see if what we are doing for our marketing is working or not.

We start by looking at the numbers that tell us how many people come to our website. We want to see if this number is getting bigger. If more people are coming, it might mean they like our ads or our product. It's good when this number grows. But if it goes down, we have to figure out why and try to fix it.

Next, we look at how many of these visitors are buying what we're selling. It's not just about getting people to our store or website. It's about making sure they find what they want and buy it. We call this "conversion." When people buy, our conversion numbers go up. This is great because it means our marketing is helping people decide to buy from us.

We also want to know how people find us. Do they come from an online search, or do they click on an ad? Knowing this helps us decide where to put our ads and how to talk to our customers. It's like finding the best path to a treasure. Once we know the path, we can use it more and make sure it's easy for people to follow.

But numbers alone don't tell us everything. They are like puzzle pieces. To see the whole picture, we put the pieces together. This means comparing our numbers over time. We look at this month, last month, and maybe even last year. By doing this, we can see if we are doing better or if we need to try harder.

Once we have all these answers, we can make better choices. If we see that one kind of ad is bringing a lot of people to our website, we might decide to use that kind of ad more. Or if we notice that people are visiting our website but not buying, we might try to make our website easier to use or our product easier to buy.

Sometimes, we might find that some things just don't work. It's okay. It's part of learning. When something doesn't work, we stop doing it. Then we use what we've learned to try new things. This helps us to spend our time and money on what really helps our business grow.

It's important to remember that making decisions with data is not just a one-time thing. It's something we do all the time. Every day, every week, every month. We keep looking at our numbers, keep asking questions, and keep learning. This way, we get better at understanding what our customers want and how we can give it to them.

In the end, what matters is that we use our numbers to help our business do well. We want more people to know about us, more people to like what we sell, and more people to buy from us. By using data to make choices, we can help make sure this happens. It's a little like being a detective. We look for clues in our numbers and use them to solve the mystery of how to make our business a success.

And remember, we're not alone in this. There are tools and people who can help us understand our data. We can use computer programs to help sort and make sense of our numbers. And if we ever get stuck, there are people who are really good at this kind of detective work. We can ask them for help to make sure we're doing the best for our business.

So let's take our time. Let's look at each number, understand what it's telling us, and use that understanding to make good decisions. This way, we're not just guessing; we're using real information to help our business grow. And that's how we make our marketing work for us.

Continuous Improvement and SEO Maintenance

Let's talk about keeping your SEO on top. SEO isn't a one-time thing. It's like taking care of a garden. You can't just plant seeds and walk away. You need to water the plants, pull out the weeds, and check on them to make sure they grow well. With SEO, your website is the garden. You have to keep working on it to make it better all the time. This means checking your website, updating it, and making sure everything is working as it should.

First, let's be clear about one thing. SEO changes a lot. Search engines like Google change their rules often. So, what worked for your website last year might not work this year. That's why you need to keep an eye on your SEO. It's a big deal because if you don't, your website might not show up when people search for things you talk about or sell.

Now, you might be thinking, "What do I need to do to keep my SEO good?" Well, my friend, you need a checklist. A maintenance checklist. This is a list of things you do for your website regularly. It's like a to-do list for your site's SEO health. Let's walk through this checklist together.

First on the list is checking your website's speed. A fast website is important. Think about it. When you visit a website and it's slow, do you wait? Probably not. You leave and go somewhere else. Your visitors are the same. They want fast websites. So you need to check if your site loads quickly. If it doesn't, you need to figure out what's making it slow and fix it.

Next up is looking at your content. Is it still good? Does it match what people are searching for now? Sometimes things change. Maybe people use different words to search for things. Maybe there's new information or products. You need to make sure your content is fresh and useful.

Now let's talk about links. Links on your website need to work. If someone clicks on a link and it doesn't go anywhere, that's bad. It makes people frustrated and they might not come back. You need to check all your links to make sure they take people where they're supposed to go.

Don't forget about new things on your website. Maybe you added new pages or posts. You have to check that you did your SEO work on those too. Every new piece of content needs to be looked at to make sure it's following your SEO rules.

Keywords are words or phrases people use to search for things. You need to make sure you're using the right keywords on your website. Sometimes the keywords people use can change. Or maybe there are new keywords you hadn't thought about before. You need to research and update your keywords regularly.

Another check is for updates. Just like your phone needs updates, so does your website. This could be your website's platform, like WordPress, or the plugins you use. These updates can help your website work better and stay secure. It's important to keep everything up to date.

One more thing to do is to look at how people use your website. You want to see what pages they visit, how long they stay, and if they do what you want them to do, like buy something or sign up for your newsletter. This information can tell you a lot about what's working and what's not.

Last but not least, keep learning about SEO. It's always changing, and there's always new stuff to know. Read about it, watch videos, or take classes. The more you know, the better you can do.

So, there you have it. A maintenance checklist for your SEO. It might seem like a lot, but it's worth it. Keeping your SEO up to date helps your website show up when people search for things. And that can mean more visitors, and maybe even more customers.

Remember, this is all about making your website the best it can be. You want people to find you, like what they see, and come back. Taking care of your SEO is a big part of that. So use this checklist, keep learning, and keep improving. It's an ongoing thing, but it's an important thing.

Now you've got a clear plan. A checklist to help you keep your SEO sharp. You've got this. Keep your website fast, your content fresh, your links working, and everything up to date. Check on how people use your site and learn as much as you can about SEO. Do these things, and you'll be on your way to keeping your website's SEO in tip-top shape.

Demonstrating Value and ROI to Stakeholders

When it comes to local marketing, it's not just about getting the word out. It's about making sure the effort pays off. It's time to talk about how to show the real worth of your hard work to the people who matter most in your business. These people are your stakeholders. They could be your partners, investors, or even your team members. They all have a stake in the success of your business.

First, we need to understand what stakeholders care about. Think about it. They want to know that the resources they put in, like time, money, or effort, are helping the business grow. They need to see numbers and facts that prove your marketing is working. This is where you need to be clear and tell them about your success in a way that they will get it.

Now, let's break down how to communicate SEO value. SEO stands for Search Engine Optimization. It's a way to help your business show up online when people search for things you offer. To show its value, you need to collect data. This data might be how many people visit your website, how long they stay, and what they do while they're there. You also want to see if these visits lead to sales. Then, you need to put this information together in a report that's easy to understand. Use simple charts and lists to show changes over time. This way, stakeholders can see how things are getting better because of what you're doing.

Now, let's talk about calculating ROI, which stands for Return on Investment. Calculating ROI helps you understand if the money you spend on marketing is making more money for your business. To do this, you need to figure out how much you spent on your marketing. This includes everything like ads, tools, and even the time you spend. Then, you need to find out how much you made from these efforts. You can find this out by tracking sales that came from people visiting your site or using special codes on your ads. Subtract the money you spent from the money you made. If you have more money after, that means you have a positive ROI, which is great news.

When presenting SEO and marketing results to stakeholders, keep things simple. Use clear words and avoid business talk that might confuse them. Show the link between what you did and how it made the business better. For instance, if more people visited your site and then bought something, point this out. Say, "We got 100 more website visitors last month, and our sales went up by 10%. This means our new ads are working."

In the end, it's all about showing that the marketing you're doing is worth it. This means taking the time to collect the right data, analyze it, and share it in a way that's clear and to the point. By doing this, you make sure everyone understands and appreciates the hard work you're doing to help the business succeed. You also set a strong foundation for making better decisions in the future. When stakeholders see the real value of your marketing, they will support your efforts even more. And that's a win for everyone.

So, remember, track your results, know your numbers, and share your success. This is how you show the real power of your marketing and keep your business growing strong.

Recap: Mastering Measurement and ROI

Let us take a deep breath and step back to take a good look at what we've talked about. This chapter has been a journey through the world of tracking success and measuring ROI. We've explored different ways to understand if our local marketing is working. It's time to put those ideas into practice. And that's what we'll do now.

First of all, remember the goals and KPIs we set earlier? Those were not just any goals. They were clear signs that we're on the right track. They tell us if we're doing well or if we need to make changes. Like a map for a treasure hunt, they guide us to where we want to go.

Now, think about the tools for tracking our performance. We learned about some neat software that can help us see how our local SEO is doing. It's like having a pair of glasses when your vision is blurry. With these tools, you can see clearly how your business is doing online.

But what do we do with all the numbers these tools give us? We learned some ways to make sense of the data. It's like looking at a picture and trying to understand the story it tells. When we understand the story behind the numbers, we can make smart choices for our business.

Remember, SEO isn't something you do just once. It needs care, like a garden. We talked about how to keep our SEO strong with regular checks and updates. This helps our business stay fresh and relevant online.

We also learned how to show others the value of our SEO work. If we've done well, we want people to know about it. We learned some ways to calculate ROI. This tells us how much money we've made compared to how much we spent.

Here's a simple action plan you can follow to use everything we've talked about:

- Set your goals. Think about what you want for your business. More visitors? More sales? Write these goals down.
- Choose your KPIs. Pick some clear signs that will show you're reaching your goals. These could be things like how many people visit your website or how many buy something.
- Get your tools ready. Find a tracking tool that works for you and set it up. Make sure it's tracking the right things for your goals.
- Check your numbers. Regularly look at your data. Try to see the story it's telling. Is your business growing? Are more people visiting your website? Try to figure out why.
- Keep your SEO fresh. Every so often, check your website to make sure everything's working well. Update things if needed.
- Show your work. When your SEO does well, tell people about it. Use simple numbers to show how your efforts are helping the business make more money.

Keep this action plan handy. Use it to guide your steps as you work on your local marketing. If you do these things, you will see your business grow. And that's what we all want, isn't it?

Remember to take it step by step. Be patient and keep learning. Marketing is a big world with many paths. But with a clear map, a sharp eye, and a will to keep going, you'll find your way. Your business will thank you for it.

And that's it. We've covered a lot, but it's just the beginning. With these tools and knowledge, you're ready to make your local marketing efforts shine. Go out there and track your success. Measure your ROI. Do this, and you'll see your business grow and thrive.

Consolidation of Core Concepts

We've come a long way together. We've dived deep into the world of SEO and local marketing, unearthing treasures of knowledge that can transform the way you approach online presence for your business. It's time to reflect on the key lessons we've shared, to ensure they're not just words on a page but tools in your toolbox, ready for action.

The core of SEO is simple. It's about making sure your website shows up when people search for what you offer. Think of search engines like matchmakers. They want to introduce users to the perfect websites for their needs. To do this, your website needs to speak the language of these matchmakers. This means using the right words, the same words people type into search bars when they're looking for businesses like yours.

But it's not just about words. Your website needs to load fast, be easy to use, and shine on any device, especially mobile phones. Why? Because that's where a lot of people do their searching. And if your website is tough to use on a phone, people will leave. Search engines see this. They notice when people don't stay on your site. This tells them maybe your website isn't that great after all, and they'll introduce it to fewer people as a result.

Local marketing, on the other hand, is about focusing on customers near you. It's about making sure that when someone says "I need something near me," your business comes to mind. This means claiming your spot on maps and local listings, making sure your address, phone number, and hours are up to date. It's like telling the world, "We're here, we're open, and we're ready to serve you."

Reviews are your best friend in local marketing. They're like personal recommendations from your customers to the world. The more good reviews you have, the more likely someone is to choose your business over another. So encourage happy customers to leave their thoughts online. Make it easy for them. Remember, a few kind words from them can lead to many more customers walking through your door.

Now, let's talk links. Not just any links, though. Quality ones that make sense. When trustworthy websites link to yours, it's like getting a thumbs-up from the cool kids in school. Search engines see this and think, "Wow, this site must be good if they're linking to it." But be careful, not all links are helpful. Bad ones can drag you down. Like a bad rumor, they can make search engines question your website's trustworthiness.

Content is your secret weapon. It's not just about selling your product or service. It's about helping people, answering their questions, and giving them value, even if they don't buy right then. This builds trust. People come back to places they trust. And when they're ready to buy, they'll think of you.

We cannot forget about keywords. These are the signposts that guide people to your website. You need to know what words people use when they search for what you offer. Then, use those words on your site. But it's not just about stuffing those words in anywhere. They need to fit naturally. It's like cooking; the right ingredients can make a dish delicious, but too much of one thing and it's ruined.

Remember to keep your website fresh, too. This means updating your content regularly. When you do, it's a signal to search engines that your site is alive, kicking, and keeping up with the times. This keeps you on their radar.

Finally, social media. It's not just for sharing funny videos and what you had for lunch. It's an SEO tool, too. When you're active on social media, engaging with your community, and sharing helpful content, you create a buzz. Search engines hear this buzz. It tells them you're relevant, you're popular, and you're worth paying attention to.

These concepts aren't just ideas. They're the foundation of a strong online presence. They're the steps to making sure your website and your business stand out in the crowded online marketplace. Use them well, and you'll see the difference they can make.

So, keep these lessons close. Apply them. Make them part of your everyday strategy, and watch as your business grows from a quiet spot on the web to a loud, bustling hub that attracts customers day and night. It's all in your hands now. Make it work for you.

The Call to Continuous Growth

Life, much like business, never stands still. Growth is a vital part of our journey. You've learned a lot about SEO and local marketing. Now the real work begins. Applying these strategies to your business is where change happens. It's about taking action. Every day is a chance to do something great with your business. Let's talk about that.

It's easy to read a book. It's harder to do the work. But you're not looking for easy. You're looking for impact. Your business is your dream turned real. Dreams grow when fed with effort and smart strategies. You have the strategies. Now, bring the effort. It's time to roll up your sleeves. Let's make your business better together.

Start with what you know. You've learned to find the right keywords. Use them. Write content that helps people. Make your website a place people want to visit. Then, look at your business listings. Are they complete? Are they accurate? Fix them if they're not. This is how you get found. This is how you grow.

Next, talk to your customers. Ask for reviews. Good reviews make a difference. They help others trust you. But also, learn from bad reviews. They are chances to improve. Use them. Every review is a step toward growth. Do not ignore them. They are too valuable.

Growth is never a quick race. It's a marathon. It's long. It's hard. But it's worth it. Take it one step at a time. Do one thing for your business every day. Make one change. Try one new idea. This keeps you moving forward. This is how you grow. This is how you succeed.

Remember, the world changes fast. Keep learning. SEO changes. Marketing changes. Stay up to date. Read blogs. Watch videos. Talk to experts. Never stop learning. This keeps you ahead. This keeps you growing. Your business needs this. It needs your best ideas. It needs your action.

And don't do it all alone. Find others like you. Join groups. Share ideas. Get feedback. Help others. When you help, you also learn. This is how community works. It lifts everyone up. It pushes everyone forward. Be a part of that. Your business will thank you for it.

Last, set goals. Small goals. Big goals. It doesn't matter. Just have goals. They give you direction. They give you purpose. When you reach a goal, set another. Keep moving. Keep growing. This is how greatness happens. This is how your business becomes what you dream it can be.

So, what's your next step? It's to take everything you've learned and put it into action. Revisit your notes. Look at your plans. Make the changes that will grow your business. You have the knowledge. You have the tools. Now, show the world what you can do. Keep growing. Keep striving. Keep succeeding. Your business depends on it. And so do you.

Comprehensive Action Plan

Putting a plan into action can often be the difference between success and mere ideas. You've learned a lot about strategies, but knowing isn't the same as doing. Now is the time to take those strategies you've absorbed and start applying them. Let's talk about how to do this, step by step, so you can see real change.

First things first, you need to have a clear goal. This goal should be something you can see, touch, and know when you've achieved it. For example, if your business needs more customers, your goal might be to get 10 new customers in the next month. It's simple, it's clear, and you'll know when you get there. Keep your goal in your mind as we walk through this action plan.

Your action plan begins with your website. Take a look at it as if you were a customer. Does it load quickly? Can people find what they need without getting lost? Make sure your website is easy to use. This means big buttons, simple words, and clear directions on what to do next. If you need to make changes, write down exactly what needs to be done and by when. Maybe you need to add a contact form or change some pictures. Get specific about what needs to change, then do it.

SEO is our next stop. You've got to make sure people can find you when they search online. Start with keywords. These are like little clues that lead people to your website. Think about what words your customers might use to find your business. Write them down. Then, sprinkle these words all over your website like magic dust. But do it in a way that feels normal and easy to read.

But SEO isn't just about keywords. It's also about making friends with other websites. This means finding websites that will link back to you. These are called backlinks, and they help show that your website is important. Reach out to other businesses or blogs and ask if they can link to your site. Offer to do the same for them. This helps everyone.

Now, let's talk about content. Content is like the food you feed your website to keep it healthy and growing. You need to create content that people want to read. This could be blog posts, videos, or even pictures. But remember, it has to be useful to your customers. Write about things they care about. If you sell shoes, maybe you write about the best ways to keep them clean or the latest shoe trends. Plan to make one new piece of content each week. Write down your ideas and when you will make them happen.

Let's not forget social media. This is where you can talk to your customers. You can share your new content here and start conversations. Choose one or two social media platforms where you know your customers hang out. Maybe it's Facebook or Instagram. Post something every day. It could be a picture, a question, or even just a hello. Write down a list of what you will post each day.

Reviews are gold. Ask your happy customers to leave a review. This shows other people that your business is good. You could send a friendly email after someone buys something, asking them to write a review. Make it easy for them. Maybe you include a link right to where they need to go to leave that review. Keep track of who you've asked and who has left a review.

Last but not least, measure what you're doing. You need to see what's working and what's not. This means looking at numbers. How many people visit your website? How many people buy something? Use tools like Google Analytics to keep an eye on these numbers. Every month, take some time to look at what the numbers are telling you. Write down what they say and think about what you might need to change.

This action plan is meant to turn your knowledge into real steps that lead to real results. Each part of the plan has things you need to do and things you need to keep track of. Write everything down. Make a checklist if that helps you. Do one thing at a time and cross it off the list when it's done.

Remember, this isn't a one-time thing. You need to keep feeding your business with these steps. Keep updating your website. Keep finding keywords. Keep making content. Keep posting on social media. Keep asking for reviews. And keep looking at your numbers.

You've got the knowledge. Now use it. Take these steps and put them into action. Your business depends on it. And you can do it. One step at a time, one day at a time. Start now. You've got a plan, and it's time to make it happen.

The Next Steps Forward

You've made it through a journey. We've covered a lot, right? From learning what SEO is to mapping out strategies specific to local marketing. You feel more confident, sure of your next steps. This is the end of the book, but it's only the beginning for you and your business. What's next? Well, it's time to put all that knowledge into action. You see, knowing things is great, but doing them is what really counts. It's like having a recipe for a cake. You could know every ingredient by heart, but you won't have a cake until you mix them all together and bake it. Let's talk about taking action. It's the most important part. It's the difference between dreaming about success and actually making it happen. You've learned so much. Now, it's time to use it. Roll up your sleeves. Get ready. But maybe you're thinking, "Where do I start?" Start with the first step. Just one small step. Maybe it's improving your website, or maybe it's getting your business on more local listings. You don't have to do everything at once. Take it one step at a time. You might also be thinking, "What if I need help?" That's okay. Everyone needs help sometimes. It's smart to ask for it. That's where Digileadgenbot comes in. They're ready to help you take those steps. They can guide you, answer your questions, and give you that extra push towards your goals. Here's what you can do. Reach out. Send an email to serge@digileadgenbot.com. Say hello. Tell Serge about your business. Share what you've learned from this book. And then, ask for help with what you're stuck on. Maybe you need more leads. Maybe you want to make more sales. Or, maybe you want your brand to be the one everyone knows and trusts. Digileadgenbot has these special packages. They call them the Grand Slam offers. They're like a secret weapon for your business. You can get your business listed in all the right places. Imagine 50, 100, even 300 local citations. That means when people search for what you do, they find you. Not just once, but over and over. This boosts your chances of making sales. And there's more. You can get backlinks. These are like votes for your website that say, "Hey, this is a good place." The more you have, the more likely people are to find you. You can get 5, 10, 20, or even 50 each month. That's a lot of votes! Why do you need this? Because it's about more than just being online. It's about being seen. It's about being chosen. It's about growing your business into something amazing. This is your time. Your moment. So, take that next step. Reach out to Digileadgenbot. Tell them you're ready. Ready for more leads. Ready for more sales. Ready to make your brand stand out. You can do this. You're not alone. Remember, every big journey starts with a single step. You've taken many steps already by learning and growing. Now, take the next one. Contact Serge. Start turning your knowledge into action. Into results. Into a future where your business is booming, and you're the one they all come to. It's time to take the leap. Are you in? Let's do this. Together.

Additional Resources for Success

Getting to grips with what has been taught is just the start. To really fly, you need the right tools in your kit. Think of these tools as friends who are there to give you a lift when you need it. They won't do the work for you, but they're there to help when you're ready to roll up your sleeves and get your hands dirty. Here's a list of resources to help you soar.

First up, books. Books are like treasure chests. Each one you open can fill your head with golden ideas. There are loads of books out there about SEO and local marketing. Start with the ones that most people say are good. Then, find the ones that speak to you and your business.

Next, we have websites and blogs. These are like your morning news. They keep you in the loop with what's new and what's changing. SEO and marketing are always changing. It's like the weather. So stay sharp and keep learning from the experts who write these blogs. You can find a lot of great ones with a quick search on the internet.

Also, consider online courses. These are like classrooms where you can learn at your own pace. You can start and stop whenever you like. There are plenty out there, from beginners to advanced. Pick the ones that fit what you need to learn next.

Don't forget about tools and software. These are like your magic wands. They help you do things faster and better. For SEO, you might need tools to find the right keywords or to see how your website is doing. And for local marketing, you might need tools to help you manage your social media or to send out emails to your customers. The right tool can make a big job feel much, much easier.

Podcasts and webinars can be handy, too. Think of them as your talk radio. They're full of tips and interviews with people who've been where you are now. They can be a great way to learn while you're doing other things like driving or working out.

Remember forums and online communities as well. These are like your neighborhood barbecues. Everyone shares their stories, and you can learn a lot from what worked for them or what didn't. And you can ask questions, too. It's a great way to get help and to help others.

Now, let me tell you about a secret weapon. Mentors and coaches. They're like personal trainers for your business brain. They can push you to do more than you thought you could. If you can find a good one, they can change the game for you.

Finally, don't forget about networking. It's like the family you choose. The more people you know, the more you can learn and share. And sometimes, the people you meet can open doors for you that you didn't even know were there.

All of these resources are waiting for you. They're there to help you build on what you've learned. They're there to help you keep growing and to keep getting better at what you do. So, go on. Reach out and grab them. Use them to climb higher and to reach your dreams. Remember, where you are right now is just the beginning.

The next step is to take what you've learned and use it. Use it to make your business shine. And if ever you feel stuck, just look around at all the resources out there. Reach out for them. They're there for you.

If you want to get in touch or if you have questions, you can always reach me at serge@digileadgenbot.com. Or, if you like, come and check out my blog at https://medium.com/@digileadgenbot and my YouTube channel at https://www.youtube.com/@DigiLeadGenBot. There you'll find more tips and tricks to keep your business moving forward.

Remember, the journey of a thousand miles starts with a single step. And now, you've got a whole list of steps to take you even further. The sky's the limit. So keep reaching, keep growing, and keep pushing forward. Your success is out there, just waiting for you to grab it.

www.ingramcontent.com/pod-product-compliance
Lightning Source LLC
LaVergne TN
LVHW051240050326
832903LV00028B/2496